PROF. SHAKEEL AHMAD

DEPARTMENT OF LAW
ALIGARH MUSLIM UNIVERSITY
ALIGARH

I0504157

Certificate

It gives me an immense pleasure to certify that **Mr. Mohd Noveed Sarwer Khan** bearing Roll No.21-LL.M-16 & Enrolment No. GJ6076 student of LL.M. Final year has completed his dissertation captioned **"Role of Police in Administration of Criminal Justice System in India: An Analytical Study"** under my supervision. To the best of my knowledge, the work is suitable for the submission in partial fulfilment of the requirement of the Degree of Master of Laws.

I wish him all the success for his future endeavour.

Prof (Dr.) Shakeel Ahmad

i

𝔇eclaration by Candidate

I, **Mohd Noveed Sarwer Khan**, hereby declare that this dissertation titled **"Role of Police in Administration of Criminal Justice System in India: An Analytical Study"** is the result of my own research undertaken under the guidance of *Prof. [Dr]. Shakeel Ahmad, Faculty of law Aligarh Muslim University.* It has not previously formed the basis for the award of any degree, diploma, or certificate of this Institute or of any other institute or university. I have duly acknowledged all the sources used by me in the preparation and writing of this dissertation.

Mohd Noveed Sarwer Khan
LLM. II Year
Faculty of Law
Aligarh Muslim University

Acknowledgement

*I bow to the **Almighty Allah;** the Merciful, the Benevolent, and the Compassionate, who blessed me with all the vigour when and where I felt need and whenever, to embark upon this task and always guided me at the path of virtue, honesty and fear of Him.*

*At the onset I would like to record my gratitude to my supervisor, **Prof. (Dr.) SHAKEEL AHMAD,** who right from choosing this topic to the last stage in its completion rendered every possible assistance. Without his guidance, constructive criticism and valuable discussion this dissertation would not have reached its culmination. I attribute the level of my work to his encouragement and effort and appreciate all that he did to make this experience productive and stimulating. I am indebted to him for patiently bearing me all those times when I could not meet his set time limits.*

*I have no words to express my sincere gratitude to the continuous struggle and immense support of my Respected Father **MR. TALAT SARWER KHAN** and my Beloved Mother **Mrs. SHAHNAZ AKHTAR** for providing me the opportunity to make this academic pursuit.*

*I would like to thank my dear siblings, **Dr. Subhat, Dr.Wajida. Dr.Muskan, Miss.Tania,** for their unconditional love and Encouragement. I shower my love and affection to my Niece **Eshal Fatima.** And special thanks to **Nadeem Shah, Dr.Obaid** for their constant support and assistance whenever needed.*

*I would like to heartily thank some of the special human beings & Friends **Dr.Shaeyuq shah, Dr.Irfan Jafri, Zakia khan, Muskeen Ali, Zia-ul-haq, Ather Ayoub, Tasneem Kawoos Abu Shahma, Adv.Md.Waseem, Bilal bhatt, Md.Faisal, Irfan Ahmad, Dr.Haroon Rashid, Ahrar khan, Shahid, Anzar Shabir, Dr.Jameel Ahmad, Dr.Zaheer Abbas, Dr.Makhan Din, Naveed Raza, Amir kohli, Alyas Ch, Iftikar ahmad. Dr.Inzamam, Wajid CH, Er.Nadeem, Er.Irfan ul Haq, Fahad Abdullah, Umed Ali, Faisal Yaseen, Inzamam, Ruksana, Tazeen,** for their valuable advices & bearing with me lengthy discussion & made sure that I stay motivated & focused throughout my research. Their contribution is highly commendable.*

*I would also like thank my Uncles, **Qateel khan, Hamayun khan, Iqbal Khan, Zaheer khan.** and my beloved cousins, **Abrar khan, Nafeez khan, Salma, Faraz, Nobeel, Zara, Mehar, Zeeshan, Hameeza, Madiha, Adeeba ,Mehreen, Azeem khan.***

List of Abbreviations:

1	IPC	Indian Penal Code
2	CrPC	Code of Criminal Procedure
3	SC	Supreme Court
4	STF	Special Task Force
5	CBI	Central Bureau of Investigation
6	NHRC	National Human Rights Commission
7	NPC	National Police Commission
8	NCRB	National Crime Records Bureau
9	UNDP	United Nations Development Programme
10	SHO	Station House Officer
11	FIR	First Information Report
12	DNA	Deoxyribonucleic Acid
13	NIA	National Investigation Agency
14	SP	Superintendent of Police
15	DSP	Deputy Superintendent of Police
16	SI	Sub Inspector
17	ASI	Assistant Sub Inspector
18	DGP	Director General of Police
19	DIG	Deputy Inspector General
20	IGP	Inspector General of Police
21	CRPF	Central Reserve Police Force
22	BSF	Border Security Force
23	ITBP	Indo Tibetan Border Police
24	CISF	Central Industrial Security Force
25	SSB	Sashastra Seema Bal

TABLE OF CONTENTS

Chapter 1: Introduction 1

1: Significance of the topic ....

2. Problem ....

3.Objective of study ....

4: Hypotheses ....

5: Research Methodology ..

6: Literature Review...

Chapter 2: The Police System in India 15

1: Introduction...

2: Origin of Police..

3: Development of Police Organization ....

4: Historical survey and evolution of Police Force in India ....

5: The Police Set-Up in India...

    1.   Police Organisation under the State Government............................

    2.   Police Organisation Under Central Government.............................

    3.   Police commissioners ....

Chapter 3: Role of Police In India: With SpecialReference To Present Criminal Justice System27

1: Criminal Justice system & its Process..

2: Role of Police towards Criminal Justice System...

3: Legal Functioning of Police ....

4: Problems Faced by the Police...

Chapter 4: The Process and Procedure of Investigation................................. 54

1: Introduction..

2: The process and procedure of investigation..

3: Legal Provisions of CRPC Related to Investigation ....

4: Abuses of Power by Police during Investigation..

5: Brutality of Police ....

5: Relevant cases with regard to Investigation...

Chapter 5: Recommendation of Various Committees on Police Reforms 65

1: Gore Committee on Police Training 1971 – 1973 ....

2: National Police Commission (NPC) 1977–1981 ....

3: Ribeiro Committee on Police Reforms (1998-1999) ....

4: Padmanabhaiah Committee on Police Reforms (2000)..

5: Malimath Committee on Reforms of Criminal Justice System (2001–2003) ....

6: Police Act Drafting Committee (2005–2006)..

Chapter 6: Judicial Contribution to The Police System in India: And A Case Study Of The Prakash Singh 71

Case 1: Introduction to Judicial Contribution to Police System ....

2: Role of the Judiciary in Police Reform in India ....

3: Analysis of the Prakash Singh Case..

4: Assessment of Police Reforms in India after the Prakash Singh Case...................................

5: Supreme Court's directives for avoidance of Custodial crime..

6: Judicial Response on violation of human rights by Police..

Chapter-7 Legal Provisions Relating to Police...79

1: The Police Act, 1861...

2: The Police Act 1888..

3: The Police (Incitement to Disaffection) Act, 1922 ....

4: The Police Act, 1949...

5: The Delhi Special Police Establishment Act 1946...

Chapter 8: Conclusion and Suggestions, Recommendations...89

Bibliography 100

Abstract

The administration of India's criminal justice system and the function of police are both examined in this analytical study. The overview of the Indian police system's structure and organisation, including its legal foundation and operational procedures, comes first. The paper then explores the methodology and practise of police investigations, highlighting pertinent legal requirements and police power abuses throughout the course of investigations.

The study also looks at the suggestions made by several committees, including the Gore Committee, the National Police Commission, the Ribeiro Committee, the Padmanabhaiah Committee, and the Malimath Committee, regarding police reforms in India.

The analysis of the historic Prakash Singh case and the Supreme Court's orders for police reform to stop custody crimes and human rights abuses serve as the study's conclusion. Overall, this study offers insightful information about the difficulties and opportunities faced by the police in India's administration of the criminal justice system.

CHAPTER 1
INTRODUCTION

The police department continues to be one of culture's most influential institutions. As a consequence, law enforcement officers are the regime's most visible participants. When a citizen is in distress, danger, disaster, or difficulty and is uncertain what to do or whom to call, the law enforcement and a cop are the most appropriate and likable entity and individual to reach. The police can be the most approachable, engaging, and diverse organization of every community[1].

Their positions, tasks, and responsibilities in community are normal to be diverse and broad and difficult, knotty, and dynamic on the other side. In general, the police are required to fulfil two functions in a society: the protection of law and the maintenance of order. However, the repercussions of these two tasks are various, necessitating the development of a comprehensive inventory of the police organization's duties, abilities, forces, positions, and obligations. Police is the function of the executive division of government tasked with the responsibility of maintaining public peace and tranquillity, promoting public health, protection, and morality, and preventing, detecting, and punishing offenses.

The 1861 Police Act[2] is a notable piece of legislation that specifies police officers' responsibilities and jurisdiction. It is important to reconfigure the officers to investigate it a more powerful tool for crime reduction and identification," the Act's preamble states. The Indian legal framework granted a great deal of autonomy to the country's inhabitants.

Regrettably, not everybody is conscious of the military. As an Indian resident, it is important that you are informed of the regional laws and privileges. Apart from straightforward laws and rights, there are additional fundamental rules and rights that must be understood by all.

Article 21[3] of the Indian Constitution2 instils faith in the lives of those who are jailed, awaiting trial, or convicted. These people should be handled humane manner and in

---

[1]   Dr. C.P. Gupta (Head & Associate Professor, Apex University, Jaipur) And Rekha Khandelwal (Research Scholar, Rajasthan University, Jaipur)
[2]   Rao, P. Hari. "The Indian Police Act (Act V of 1861)." (1927).
[3]   Bakshi, Parvinrai Mulwantrai, and Subhash C. Kashyap. The constitution of India. Universal Law Publishing, 1982

accordance with the law. The Apex Court ruled in **Menaka Gandhi v. Union of India**[4] that the State, and specifically the security as its primary security department's body, have an indisputable obligation to carry criminals to justice. Nonetheless, the legislation and practice used by the State to accomplish this admirable social purpose shall adhere to humane standards.

As a result, the State's procedure must be legal, equal, and logical. As a result, another concept of 'Police' may be derived from the preamble: Police is a tool whose aim is to deter and detect crime. Since 1860, senior police officials were recruited in two ways: first, by selection of officers from the British Army; and second, through election from among the younger sons of the UK's landed gentry[5]. All of these modes of transport were phased down in 1893. Officer selection was now conducted by a joint professional test conducted in London and open to only Europeans.

It was later accessible to Indians as well. Today, the Union Public Service Commission conducts regular recruitment via the Combined Civil Services Review. The All India Services are stated in Article 312 of the Indian Constitution. Probationers are subjected to extremely rigorous basic instruction in studies, weaponry, and other tasks.

The police force is a state matter, as per the Constitution. The state police manual contains laws, legislation, and instructions for the police. In India, the organizational framework of police forces is fairly standardized throughout the country's regions. The term "Director General of Police" refers to the head of a nation's law enforcement (DGP). Areas, levels, and divisions are additional subdivisions of a territory.

A Superintendent of Police leads the district department (SP). The selection of regions forms a network, which is headed by a Deputy Inspector General (DIG). Locations are divided into two or three sections, each led by an officer holding the position of Inspector General of Police (IG). Additionally, districts are divided into loops and security departments each of which is headed by a certain kind of policeman. Additionally, the district police are divided into two department office spaces: civil and military officers. The former is mainly responsible for crime prevention, whilst the latter is responsible for law and order and serves as the district's standby police force in the event of an emergency.

---

4   AIR 1978 SC 597
5   P.D. SHARMA, CRIMINAL JUSTICE SYSTEM, 50, (Rawat Publications, Jaipur, 1998)

The Indian Police force and organization as it now exists was mostly founded on a 131-yearold Act, the 1861 Police Act[6]. Over a 90-year timeframe, the police's operation has been analysed twice at the All India level.

The first was the Indian Commission, which was established in 1902-03 under the British rule, and the second was the National Police Commission, which was established in 1977. They discovered that police were inefficient, deficient in preparation and organization, lacking in public affairs, welfare measures, and mechanisms for resolving complaints, among other deficiencies, and that they were widely viewed as corrupt and authoritarian. Even after liberation, we lacked a more effective method of law enforcement.

There is also a need for a readjustment of the police's mindset and strategy. The police function has changed constantly and continues to need modification. It is critical to turn it into a competent service rather than one that merely follows the authority's instructions mindlessly[7].

Certain facets of the police force, such as preparation, ethics, civic conduct, public dealing mannerisms, criminal justice rules, police authority, and police rights, require a full redesign.

The police force's portrayal from the British period of a paan-chewing, impolite, violent, and bully in khaki needs to be updated. Indeed, the police force's actual condition requires repair, from becoming underfunded, short-staffed, overburdened, exhausted, demoralized, insufficiently prepared and fitted, and exposed to political intervention. Additionally, in a democratic country, citizens have a right to know if the police defend them[8].

The public's confidence is critical for the police to operate efficiently, and is measured by the level of confidence and reverence accorded to the police. Police must recognize that their position in culture has evolved significantly over time. Conflict mediation and support to those in need consume more of their resources and energy than coping with violence and suspects do.

---

[6]   J.C. CHATURVEDI, POLICE ADMINISTRATION AND INVESTIGATION OF CRIME, 194-199, (Isha Books, Delhi, 2006)
[7]   JAMES VADACKUMCHERY, INDIAN POLICE AND MISCARRIAGE OF JUSTICE, 18, (APH Publishing Corporation, New Delhi, 1997)
[8]   RAKESH MOHAN, POLICE AND HUMAN RIGHTS, 2, (Swastika Publications, N. Delhi, 2013).

As the mission has shifted, so should the police's approach and behaviour in order to reclaim the damaged confidence, loyalty, and cooperation of the same public with whom the police are still dedicated and devoted to security.

1: Significance of the Topic

Due to the crucial role performed by the police in upholding law and order, preventing and detecting crime, and ensuring that justice is done, the role of police in the administration of the criminal justice system in India is an important issue for research. The police force is in charge of conducting investigations and gathering evidence in order to identify and apprehend criminals. It is the initial point of contact for victims and witnesses of crimes[9].

The criminal justice system in India consists of three components: the police, the judiciary, and the correctional system. The police are responsible for investigating crimes, collecting evidence, and presenting cases before the judiciary for a fair trial. Understanding the role and functions of the police in the criminal justice system is essential for ensuring justice is delivered efficiently and effectively[10].

An analytical study of the role of police in the administration of the criminal justice system in India will help to identify challenges and issues faced by the police force, as well as areas where reforms are needed to improve the efficiency and effectiveness of the police force.

The significance of working of Police in public administration is that it has the aim of establishing law and order in the society and maintenance of peace. Along with this, it aims to protect the rights of the individuals and the interest of the society on the whole as crime is considered to be a wrong against the state not only against the individual.

So, it is the duty of the State to protect its citizens and punish the wrong doers in case any offence is committed against any individual. Police is a vital organ of our society. The execution of laws is depended on this body. Police is provided with some powers and duties which are to be exercised for the maintenance of peace in the society.

---

[9] GIRIRAJ SHAH, THE INDIAN POLICE- A RETROSPECT, 9, (Himalaya Publishing House, Bombay, 1992).

[10] J.C. CHATURVEDI, POLICE ADMINISTRATION AND INVESTIGATION OF CRIME, 195, (Isha Books, Delhi, 2006)

If the powers of are misused or not used appropriately as the per the law then it leads to infringements of laws. The best interest of the accused, victims and society can be served through ensuring proper working of police administration. An efficient mechanism acts as a threat to any potential violator of law.

However, in our country Police Powers has come in for serious criticism. The problem of pendency and backlog of cases and the method by which the accused are dealt in police custody in civil as criminal cases has become a major topic of concern.

The loopholes in laws related to proper function of police administration appears to be on the verge of collapse due to various reasons for misuse of powers can be seen.

Therefore, proper function of Police is an urgent need of the present police system in order to decide the welfare of lakh of accused. It will help to enhance the faith of general public in present Police mechanism.

It is important that each and every stage of trial or arrest should be as per the law. It would save both the accused and victims from mental, psychological stress, anxiety, financial burden, and disturbing environment of peace in their family as well as in the society.

2. Problem

In an analytical study, a number of issues related to the administration of the criminal justice system in India's police force might be examined. Among the major issues are:

- **Lack of training:** One of the biggest issues the Indian police force has is a lack of adequate training. Numerous police officers lack the necessary training to handle complicated cases or to employ contemporary investigative methods, which can result in errors, false allegations, and incorrect convictions.

- **Corruption**: In India's police force, corruption is a serious issue that can result in bias, discrimination, and the abuse of authority. Further issues may arise as a result of a lack of trust between the people and the police.

- **Resources are insufficient:** The Indian police force frequently lacks the manpower, apparatus, and facilities required to perform their responsibilities efficiently. This may result in a lack of follow-up on cases, incomplete evidence gathering, and delays in investigations.

- **Human rights violations:** The Indian police force has committed several human rights breaches, such as extrajudicial executions, torture, and deaths that occurred while being held in custody. This may cause people to lose faith in the legal system and lose trust in the police.

- **Lack of accountability**: Police personnel who commit misbehaviour frequently go unpunished, which undermines public confidence in the legal system.

Overall, these issues indicate the necessity for a critical examination of the function of the police in India's administration of the criminal justice system in order to pinpoint their origins and create workable remedies[11].

A police officer's callous behaviour toward offenders can lead in more victimization of victims. Police insensitivity results in additional victimization of people who have already endured greatly as a consequence of the main victimization. Numerous studies have amply shown the detrimental effect of inadequate and disrespectful police care, especially in situations involving sexual harassment victims.

When it comes to sexual harassment victims, officers can have an active stance, not a passive one. Insensitive behaviours, such as not trusting the plaintiff's version, interrogating the victim insensitively, leaving the victim in the dark about the investigation's success, and so on, exacerbate the victim's suffering and frequently lead to the destruction of the strongest evidence towards the perpetrator. Police handle rape incidents accordingly depending on their perception of a 'ideal rape survivor' versus a 'ideal rape prosecution.'[12]

Very often, the police are seen as perpetrators of violence, or their handling of offenses is deemed callous and biased. Occasionally, information is discovered to be fabricated in order to defend the perpetrator or the offender's relatives, or authorities ignore the alleged

---

[11]   DALBIR BHARTI, POLICE AND PEOPLE, ROLE AND RESPONSIBILITIES, 68, (APH Publishing House, New Delhi, 2006).

[12]   Sir Robert Peel's Principles, OTTAWA POLICE, https://www.ottawapolice.ca/en/about-us/Peel-sPrinciples-.aspx , (last visited on April 2, 2021)

crime or do not treat it seriously, regardless of whether the case involves incest, bride burning, or kidnapping and abduction.

The 1973 Code of Criminal Procedure states that in cognizable circumstances[13], whenever a police officer perceives a danger, he or she can apprehend a suspect without a magistrate's orders or a summons.

However, in a child gang rape situation, police offered neither defences nor took any action to apprehend the suspects. Members of the family of a 12-year-old gang rape victim say they were targeted and compelled to leave their village. Police also detained only one of the three defendants, although the remaining two remain at large.

The victim and her family members were beaten by the accused and his friends, their home was looted, and they were forced to flee due to the danger to their lives. Considering the pervasive problem of victim-witness coercion and threats to the victim-safety, witnesses the Uttar Pradesh government has released a notification requiring prosecution witnesses in criminal courts to obtain yellow identification documents.

3. Objective of Study

- Analytical research of the police's function in India's administration of the criminal justice system may have the following goals:

- To analyse the role and responsibilities of the police as well as their capabilities and restrictions within the Indian criminal justice system.

- To recognise the difficulties and problems that the Indian police force has, including corruption, a lack of resources, inadequate training, and breaches of human rights.

- To evaluate the effects of these difficulties and problems on the administration of the criminal justice system in India, taking into account the system's effectiveness and efficiency, the public's confidence in it, and the protection of human rights.

---

13   Arnesh Kumar Vs. State of Bihar, AIR 2014 SC 2756

- To put up suggestions and answers to solve these problems and challenges, such as infrastructural, training, and recruitment changes, as well as steps to promote accountability and openness in the police force.

- Informing policy and decision-making in this area and helping to advance the knowledge of the function of police in India's administration of the criminal justice system

- To explain the legal functions of police system.

- To explain the jurisprudence of the working of police. .

- To explain the effects of use and misuse of powers of police.

- To analyse the data regarding the investigation with relevant cases

4: Hypothesis

- The thorough study "Role of Police in Administration of Criminal Justice System in India: An Analytical Study" investigates the function of the police in India's criminal justice system administration. The study examines different facets of the police system, including their roles, difficulties, and the legislative framework that guides their activities.

- The study opens with an overview of the role of the police in enforcing justice, preserving law and order, and preventing and investigating crimes. It emphasizes how important it is to comprehend the police's function within the larger framework of the criminal justice system.

- The following chapters explore particular facets of the police system and their functions. It talks about how police groups were founded, how they are organized, and how they interact with local and national governments.

- It examines their roles in preventing crime, conducting investigations, upholding the peace, and maintaining the safety and security of the populace. The difficulties that the police encounter in efficiently performing their jobs are also covered in this chapter.

- The text examines the legal guidelines controlling the investigation process, such as the Criminal Procedure Code, and looks at how these laws affect the police's authority, capabilities, and responsibility. It also provides information on how to improve the efficiency and efficacy of the Indian police system in terms of accountability, community relations, training, and technology improvements. The police are an important part of the criminal justice system, and are responsible for deterring crime and obeying the law, as well as protecting public safety and providing a range of services to the neighbourhood

5: Research Methodology

Research This Study. is a largely doctrinal and relies on various research, reports, research articles, books, statutory provisions, commentaries, case reporters, and statistical data available on various government websites.

Here in this research on the topic "Police role in adminstartion of criminal justice" system the various steps or stages as a plan or strategy are summarized as follows: This research is basically a descriptive as well as explanatory in nature. The jurisprudence of Powers of police is explained. Further the right and duties exercised or performed in India are analysed from point of view of various judicial pronouncements in this regard.

The following study approach is used to examine how police are managed inside India's criminal justice system:

- Descriptive research design:- I used this research methodology to describing and analysing the function of the police in India's criminal justice system. And to obtain information on the current situation of the police administration, the survey will be carried out at a given time.

- Data Gathering: - I gathered Secondary data for this research paper. I have examined in government publications, academic papers, books, and articles.

- Data Analysis: - I have gathered information from different publications, articles and books and collected statistical data from those article, and previous survey reports.

- Following this research methods, I have researched the topic and give my optimism and my opinion, and shed light on the role of police in the administration of the criminal justice system in India and provide valuable insights for potential improvements and reforms.

6: Literature Review

An overview of the body of knowledge on the administration of the criminal justice system in India and the function of the police may be found in a literature study. Several important literary topics that might be investigated include:

- ***Police powers and restrictions***: Research on police powers and restrictions can help readers comprehend the institutional and legal frameworks that influence how the police function within India's criminal justice system. Studies on the Indian Police Act[14], the Code of Criminal Procedure[15], and the Indian Constitution may fall under this category[16].

- ***Challenges and issues faced by the police force:*** The literature on these topics might help readers comprehend the practical and operational difficulties that police personnel have while doing their duties in India. Studies on human rights violations, insufficient funding, inadequate training, and corruption are a few examples of this.

- ***Public perception of the Police***: Research on how the public views the police in India can help us understand how the public's perception of the force affects their confidence in the criminal justice system. Studies on victim satisfaction, surveys of general public opinion, and community policing programmes are a few examples of this.

- ***Effectiveness and efficiency of the criminal justice system:*** The literature on these topics can help us understand how the difficulties the police force faces affect the way the criminal justice system functions as a whole. Studies on conviction rates, case pending times, and the function of the court in securing justice might all fall under this category.

---

[14] 1861
[15] 1973
[16] Girjesh Shukla, Criminology, Crime Causation, Sentencing and Rehabilitation of Victims, -Chapter 6 - Police System in India

- *Reforms and solutions*: The literature on reforms and solutions can help readers comprehend the many interventions and policy reforms that have been suggested or put into place to solve the problems the Indian police force is currently facing. Studies on police reforms, community policing programmes, and steps to improve accountability and openness in the police force might all fall under this category.

A literature review on the role of police in the criminal justice system in India can provide a comprehensive understanding of the legal, institutional, and operational frameworks that shape the role of police, as well as the challenges and issues faced by the police force and potential solutions to address them.

Writing a literature review is very important as writing it not only enhances the knowledge about the topic but also lets us to gain and demonstrate skills especially in two areas: Obtain Information: It improves the ability to scrutinize the literature available by applying the manual or computerize methods.

It also helps in identifying a set of useful books and articles. Critical Analysis: It deals with the ability to apply critical approach to identify the valid and unbiased studies/research on the particular subject. While writing literature review researcher kept in mind that:

- The study is organized and directly related with the research questions.

- Tried to synthesize the consequences into a summary of what is and is not known. Review of literature is one of the most important principles of research process which brings to light the various studies and information relating to the research subject.

A thorough study of books, academic journals, government published handbooks, websites and online literature has been made. There are number of Law books on the concept of Powers of Police.

Books have been written specifically on the subject of powers conferred to Police under Indian law and the working of the Police in beyond its reasonable parameter. Duties of police towards its citizen are also given specifically in these books. Indian Judicial System, Judicial Reforms in India.

Administration of Police being an important subject in academics and professional field as well, efforts have been made by various writers to highlight the concept of Police Power whether they are exercised properly as per the law or abused by the police.

However, there are some studies which are indirectly relevant for the present research. The study on those literatures which is directly relevant for this research reviewed is discussed herein.

Jonathan Doak's 2008 novel, *"Victims' Privileges, Civil Rights, and Criminal JusticePreconceiving the Role of Third Parties," Hart Writing, Oxford and Portland, Oregon*, sought to reconcile the human rights system with the rights of crime victims in the best possible manner. He stated in his work that survivors of personal assault crimes were not handled to the same level as victims of power abuse.

Since the state violates personal liberty as it abuses authority, some kind of civil rights defense was deemed essential.

In the case of victims of nonstate violence, an implicit assumption that the state is responsible for its topics precludes the application of human rights dialogue into the area of non-state actor offences. *Juan Carlos Ochoas., in his book "Rights of Victims of Criminal Proceedings for Serious Human Rights Violations,"* has discussed in detail the State's legal commitments in situations involving actions constituting violations of Human Rights committed by private citizens or non-state actors.

He has addressed cases resolved by the *United Nations Human Rights Committee, the CEDAW Committee, the ECTHR, and the IATHR,* among others. Juan stressed the State's duty to conduct an impartial investigation and punish the individual that harmed the enjoyment of fundamental human rights.

Juan also stressed the interdependence of' substantive human rights enforcement' and the 'nature and availability of the procedural means necessary to provide that protection.

Andrew Karmen, in his work *"Criminal Victims6—An Introduction to Victimology (2015),* Brooks/Cole Publication Company, Pacific Grove, California, has conducted a clinically rigorous examination of a variety of topics relating to crime victims.

Chapter Scheme

Chapter 1: Introduction: The administration of criminal justice in India is a complex system that involves various stakeholders, with the police playing a central role. The police serve as the primary law enforcement agency responsible for maintaining law and order, preventing crime, and investigating and apprehending criminals. Their role in the criminal justice system is crucial in ensuring public safety, upholding the rule of law, and delivering justice to the victims and society as a whole.

Chapter 2: The Indian Police System: A review of the literature and an outline of the Indian police system are provided in this chapter. It looks at the police force's historical growth and evolution as well as its administrative setup and operational efficiency under both state and federal rule. The British developed a centralized, hierarchical police force during the colonial era, which is where the Indian police system got its start. The establishment of numerous police organizations at the state and federal levels is covered in this chapter, with special emphasis on their duties and responsibilities in upholding law and order, preventing crime, and conducting criminal investigations..

Chapter 3: The Role Of The Police In India, Particularly With Regard To The Current Criminal Justice System: The role of the police in India is the main topic of this chapter, especially in light of the country's current criminal justice system. It examines the many roles played by the police in upholding law and order, stopping and looking into crimes, and helping with the overall administration of justice.

Chapter 4 : The Process and Procedure of Investigation: This chapter focuses on the steps and practices involved in a police investigation into a crime in India. From receiving information about a crime to submitting the investigation report, it gives a general picture of the investigation procedure. The essential processes in the investigation process are described in the chapter, including the initial response to the crime site, securing the area, gathering and preserving evidence, interviewing witnesses, questioning suspects, and analyzing the gathered data. The chapter also discusses the laws that regulate investigations in India, including the Criminal Procedure Code (CrPC), which specifies the authorities and duties of the police.

Chapter 5; Recommendation of various committees on Police reform: This chapter looks at the suggestions made for police reform in India by various committees and commissions. The Gore Committee on Police Training (1971–1973).The National Police Commission (NPC) (1977–1981) The Ribeiro Committee on Police Reforms (1998–1999). Malimath Committee on Reforms of Criminal Justice System (2001-2003). The goal of the Police Act Drafting Committee (2005–2006) was to create a new national model police act.And recommendations of other committees

Chapter: 6: Judicial Contribution To The Police System In India: And A Case Study Of The Prakash Singh Case: The judiciary's influence on the development and reform of India's police system is the main topic of this chapter. In order to maintain police accountability, professionalism, and protection of human rights, it examines the judicial contributions to formulating principles, rules, and directives. Additionally, a case study of the famous Prakash Singh case, which had a major influence on police reforms in India, is presented.

Chapter-7 Legal Provisions Relating To Police: The laws in India that control how the police operate and what authority and duties they have are the main subject of this chapter. The Criminal Procedure Code (CrPC) and Indian Penal Code (IPC), as well as other laws and regulations pertaining to law enforcement, are covered in this chapter. The chapter also looks at the sections of the Indian Penal Code (IPC) and the Criminal Procedure Code (CrPC) that identify different criminal offenses and specify penalties. And important act with regard to police

Chapter 8: Conclusion and Suggestions, Recommendations: The main conclusions and major learnings from the study are outlined in this chapter, along with ideas and proposals for further enhancing the police system. It emphasizes the historical development of the police system in India, how the police are required by law to operate, how investigations are conducted, how the judiciary is involved in police reform, and the pertinent suggestions of various committees.

CHAPTER 2
THE POLICE SYSTEM IN INDIA

1: Introduction

India's police force is made up of a vast and intricate network of municipal, state, and federal law enforcement institutions. In India, the police force is in charge of upholding law and order, stopping and investigating crime, and guaranteeing the security of the general populace. The top law enforcement organisation in India, the Indian Police Service (IPS), is in charge of organising and leading the country's police force.

Each state has a police force that is in charge of upholding law and order inside its borders at the state level. The Director General of Police (DGP), who is in charge of the general management and direction of the state's police force, is in charge of the state's police force.

The Indian Police Act, passed in 1861 during the reign of the British, governs the Indian police system. To meet their unique demands, a few of governments have still passed their own police statutes. The investigative branch and the law-and-order branch make up the bulk of the Indian police force.

The discovery and investigation of crimes fall under the purview of the investigative branch. It is led by a police officer with the rank of Deputy Commissioner of Police (DCP) or Superintendent of Police (SP).

The law-and-order branch is in charge of upholding the rule of law and preventing and suppressing crime. It is led by a police official with the title of Commissioner of Police (CP) or Deputy Inspector General of Police (DIG).

The Indian police force is facing challenges such as corruption, inadequate resources, lack of training, and human rights violations, which have impacted the effectiveness and efficiency of the criminal justice system in India. Further reforms and interventions are needed to strengthen the police system.

The policing force is charged with the responsibility of stopping and fighting crimes. They are responsible for maintaining social safety, protecting VIPs, and contributing significantly to the Nation's welfare. To carry out these functions, the officers are entrusted with broad legislative authority.

This provides the authority to seize and check individuals and their belongings. Invite them to the law enforcement department for questioning and to take any legitimate steps necessary to carry out their responsibilities.

To guarantee that the public adequately use these forces, the statute imposes a variety of limits on the cops. Through the establishment of political structures, the citizens gained control, and the government recognized their fundamental rights.

And other terms, the police's primary responsibility now is to uphold the 'legal system,' which is at the heart of every modern government Numerous factors influence the method of imposing rules, including the location, period, and conditions.

The statute cannot recommend all that law compliance officers would do. For instance, according to section 160 of the Code of Criminal Procedure, a policeman conducting an examination can summon any male over the age of 15 years to the police precinct and evaluate him in accordance with the examination It is impossible to specify all of the situations whereby an individual can be summoned to a law enforcement by an investigative policeman.

The statute has delegated authority to particular police officers. The importance of police oversight is shown by the enormous authority that police departments exert over peoples' life, freedoms, protection, and privileges.

Government agencies enable cops to order people to obey the law; they authorize agents to intercept, inspect, apprehend, cite, and charge civilians, as well as to adopt aggressive and even lethal strength if cops misuse such abilities, they risk violating the constitutional protections of the same people they are sworn to defend.

As a result, it is important that police officers be held responsible for their practices and actions. Transparency is primarily guaranteed in modern democracies by three mechanisms.

2: Origin of Police

The origins of the police system in India can be traced back to the colonial period, during the British rule. The first police force in India was established in Calcutta (now Kolkata) in 1778, followed by other major cities and towns. The police force was composed of British officers and Indian subordinates, known as *the "native police"*. The Indian Police Act of 1861 was a major milestone in the history of the police system in India, providing a legal framework for the establishment and functioning of the police force, and introducing reforms aimed at improving the effectiveness and efficiency of the police force. It also gave the police force sweeping powers to maintain law and order, prevent and detect crime, and enforce the law.

The Indian police system underwent a number of adjustments and reforms following the country's 1947 declaration of independence with the goal of modernising and elevating the status of the police force. With distinct police forces for each state and union territory and a federal system of government, the fundamental makeup of the police force is essentially unaltered.

The state was founded to protect the person and property of the individual and to preserve peace in community and the King developed a law enforcement body as the chief of state. This organization evolved structurally and functionally across culture. After the Vedas came to be accepted as the ultimate example of dharma, the principle of the legal system and the justice system has been understood to operate in India.

The *Rig Veda* allows explicit reference to criminals and robbers (taya or satayas) (taskars). Manu expanded on this definition of criminality by classifying it into eighteen distinct categories. These involved harassment, slander, stealing, burglary, adultery, crime, and gaming and betting, among other offenses. The *Ramayana* and *Mahabharata*[17] provide several examples that allude to the nature of a police structure. *Kautilya's Arthasastra* contains a thorough and intriguing account of the corrupt leadership's usage of spies.

Between the **Mauryans** and their eventual predecessors and the Muslim conquests, we learn a bit about Indian police. Following the dissolution of the Hindu kingdom, the

---

[17] 8 Karol, S. (2015). Bifurcation of the Indian Police System: Investigation Wing and Law & Order Maintenance Wing. Available at SSRN 2601997.

Afghan and Mughal leaders quickly developed their own systems of security regime in India.

On top of the current system of municipal accountability for law enforcement, the northern colonizers adopted the Arabic feudalistic institutions of the Founder and the Kotwal. With the arrival of Babar and the downfall of the last Lodi king, the bureaucracy or authority on Indian soil started to take form.

Mughal rulers, particularly the later Mughals, were intensely associated with the empire's national affairs and made every effort to build upon the *Sultanat era's* heritage. Sher Shah, for example, revolutionized tax and police administration by streamlining the *'Zamindari System'*[18] .

During the Mughal era, the changes persisted. During Akbar's reign, the regional governor was referred to as a Subedar or Nazim[19] , who was assisted by a variety of Fauzdars in administering the sub-divisions. Contemporary Police Department represents the administration's constitutional authority in contrast to the administration's armed authority. The early part of police remains shrouded in mystery. Traditionally, policing, or keeping peace and engaging with wrongdoers, was a personal affair. People are tasked with the responsibility of self-protection and the upkeep of an organized community[20] In 1860, the British established the first Police Commission and incorporated the majority of its findings into the Police Act of 1861.

Thus, the British Parliament's 1861 Policing Act established the Indian police force as it exists today. The purpose of the police force to be designed became very evident as the participants of the 1860 Police Commission were instructed to keep in mind that a police force's duties are either defensive or coercive. The police department, as well as the criminal justice framework as a whole, is established to protect and maintain the British imperial framework. The British wished to avoid a repetition in 1857.

As a result, they cautiously fortified themselves with a variety of legislations and a sizable security force. The British had purposefully created a security force that was coercive in natural world; they had also purposefully given the police an arbitrary position. It suited

---

[18]   Bandyopadhyay, Rekha. "Land system in India: A historical review." Economic and Political Weekly (1993): A149-A155.
[19]   0 Ibid
[20]   Homjedar D. Crotty, Magna Carta Myth and Reality366 (1964-65)

them well, and as a result, they made no attempt to change the policemen or boost their reputation.

The Indian government established a second police commission in 1902 after internal reforms undertaken in response to the previous committee's study in 1860 failed to yield the desired results.

On March 21, 1905, the Government of India issued directives in response to the committee's advice and altered the law enforcement department When the British abandoned India on 15 August 1947, the police structure that had been updated and strengthened in response to the Police Commission's suggestions from 1902-03 was maintained.[21] As India gained freedom in 1947, it acquired a well-defined police force that had been mostly established under British control. Since India's Constitution came into effect on 26 January 1950, the scenario shifted dramatically, with the defence of human values being one of the cop's primary duties.

Numerous States established State Police Commissions, passed State Police Acts, and collected State Police Guides in an effort to reform the police force. However, India's policing force is now governed by the 1861 Police Act and the 1902 Police Commission's guidelines. When incompetence and ineffectiveness permeated the police department, and the force was undertrained and poorly prepared for the task, the chasm between the officers and the community grew when the police became viewed as the embodiment of injustice.

To expedite the organization and overhaul the police, Lord Curzon constituted, in 1902, a second all-India police committee led by Sir H.L Fraser, Chief Commissioner of the Central Regions, with the consent of the Secretary of the State for India. It noted: The Police Department is much further from productive; it is lacking in professional development and institution; it is usually recognized as fraudulent and authoritarian and it has completely struggled to earn the public's trust and coordination.

The committee was charged with determining whether the organization, mentoring, power, and compensation of the various rank and file of district cops, both outstanding and subservient, were sufficient to ensure the maintenance of public order; Whether current accommodations guarantee that crimes are published properly; Whether the framework for

---

[21] H.C Roychoudhary, Political History of Ancient India173-174(4thEdition)

investigating offenses is susceptible to enhancement; Whether the format of quantitative yields is adequate or can be improved; Whether the Railway Police's current organization, operational activities, and relationship with the district officers Several of the Commission's significant suggestions include the following:

i.   In each region, a crime inquiry agency was to be formed, with a Deputy Inspector General of Police serving as organizational head and controlling and supervising the agency's organization and operations.

ii. The province was to be separated into many variations, each of which was to be administered by a Deputy Inspector General of Police who would be hired to facilitate him.

iii. The district's Superintendent of Police was to be bolstered. He was to be assisted by a Deputy Superintendent of Police.

iv. A completely separate and autonomous police organization to be recognized as the Railway Police was also to be established on the grounds of the territories' established authority. Calcutta, Bombay, and Madras were not only the Presidential race communities, but also the locations of India 's fastest growing European populace As a result, the law enforcement of three Presidency municipalities evolved differently than the police work of district towns and rural areas in Calcutta.

Thus, the police force as it currently exists has its origins in the establishment of the government and has developed via different stages of historical past to achieve its current condition as a necessary component of operating a government's matters.

3: Development of Police Organisation

The colonial era, under British administration, is when the Indian police organisation began to take shape. Based on the English system of policing, the British formed a centralised police force in India. British officers and Indian subordinates made up the majority of the police force, which was in charge of upholding the rule of law.

The Indian police system underwent a number of adjustments and reforms following the country's 1947 declaration of independence with the goal of modernising and elevating the status of the police force.

A significant turning point in the growth of India's police force was the Police Commission of 1949. In order to increase the effectiveness and efficiency of the police force, it suggested a number of reforms.

In the years following the Police Commission of 1949, several measures were taken to strengthen and modernize the police force in India. These included the establishment of training institutions for police officers, the introduction of modern technology and equipment, and the decentralization of police administration.

The most significant reform in the history of the Indian police system was the enactment of the Police Act of 1971, which introduced several reforms aimed at improving accountability and professionalism.

It also provided for the establishment of the *Bureau of Police Research and Development (BPRD)*, responsible for research and training in the field of policing.

With independent police forces for each state and union territory, India's police organisation is now federal in nature. The Director General of Police (DGP), who oversees the overall operation of the state's police force, is in charge of the state's police forces.

There are also specialised police units, such as the Central Reserve Police Force (CRPF), whose job it is to keep the nation's internal security and law and order.

4: Historical survey and evolution of Police force in India

India's police force has evolved since the days of the ancient kings and emperors who kept a small number of watchmen and guards to uphold law and order in their realms. However, the origins of India's current police force may be found throughout the British Empire's colonial era.

In order to safeguard their own interests and uphold law and order in the nation, the British constructed a centralised police system in India in the 19th century. In 1778, Calcutta (now Kolkata) became the first city in India to establish a police force. Other significant towns and cities soon followed.

A significant turning point in the development of India's police force was the Indian Police Act of 1861. It established a number of reforms aimed at enhancing the police force's efficacy and efficiency as well as providing a legislative foundation for the establishment and operation of the police force in the nation. The Act also provided the police broad authority to uphold the law, stop and deter crime, and enforce it.

The Indian police system underwent a number of adjustments and reforms following the country's 1947 declaration of independence with the goal of modernising and elevating the status of the police force. A significant turning point in the development of India's police force was the Police Commission of 1949. It suggested numerous changes to increase the effectiveness and effectiveness of the police force.

In the years following the Police Commission of 1949, several measures were taken to strengthen and modernize the police force in India. These included the establishment of training institutions for police officers, the introduction of modern technology and equipment, and the decentralization of police administration. Today, the police force in India is a federal structure, with separate police forces for each state and union territory. The state police forces are headed by a Director General of Police (DGP), and there are specialized police forces, such as the Central Reserve Police Force (CRPF)[22].

5: The Police Set-Up in India

The police set-up in India is a federal structure, with separate police forces for each state and union territory. The state police forces are headed by a Director General of Police (DGP) who is assisted by senior officers such as the Inspector General of Police (IGP), Deputy Inspector General of Police (DIGP), and Superintendent of Police (SP).

In addition to the state police forces, there are several specialized police forces, such as the Central Reserve Police Force (CRPF), which is responsible for maintaining internal security and law and order in the country. The CRPF is primarily deployed in areas affected by insurgency and left-wing extremism.

---

[22]   re the Indian Police a Law Unto Themselves A Rights-Based Assessment- K.S. Subramanian

Another specialised unit, the Border Security unit (BSF), is in charge of guarding India's borders with Bangladesh and Pakistan. The safeguarding of India's borders with China is the responsibility of the Indo-Tibetan Border Police (ITBP).

In addition to these, there are a number of additional specialised police units, including the National Security Guard (NSG), which is in charge of counterterrorism operations, and the Rapid Action Force (RAF), which is in charge of upholding law and order during riots and other public disturbances.

The Indian police system also consists of a number of organisations tasked with looking into particular kinds of crimes. One such organisation is the Central Bureau of Investigation (CBI), which is in charge of looking into cases of corruption, economic crimes, and significant crimes that have a national or worldwide scope[23].

Other organisations that are in charge of looking into particular kinds of crimes and preserving the nation's internal security include the Narcotics Control Bureau (NCB), the Directorate of Revenue Intelligence (DRI), and the Intelligence Bureau (IB).

1. Police Organisation under the State Government

The Director General of Police (DGP), who oversees the general management of the state police force in India, is in charge of the police organisation under the state government. Ranges, zones, districts, sub-divisions, and police stations are only a few of the organisational divisions used by the state police force.

At the district level, the Superintendent of Police (SP) is in charge of upholding the rule of law and making sure that citizens are safe and secure. The administration of police at the sub-division and police station levels is the responsibility of a number of officers, including the Deputy Superintendent of Police (DSP), Assistant Superintendent of Police (ASP), and Circle Inspector (CI).

A Station House Officer (SHO), who oversees the daily operations of the police station, is in charge of every police station. Several officers, including the Sub-Inspector (SI), Assistant Sub-Inspector (ASI), Head Constable, and Constable, support the SHO.

---

[23] Austin, Granville, The Indian Constitution Cornerstone of A Nation, Oxford University Press, Delhi, 1996, 2000.

The state's police force is in charge of upholding law and order, stopping and investigating crimes, and safeguarding the lives and property of citizens. In India, the police force is also in charge of carrying out criminal investigations and bringing offenders to justice.

In addition, the state police force is in charge of keeping the peace during important occasions like elections, religious processions, and festivals. Additionally, the state's police force supports other governmental organisations in upholding law and order in times of crisis such natural disasters and civil unrest[24].

Overall, the administration of India's criminal justice system relies heavily on the police force that is part of the state government. For the upkeep of law and order and the defence of citizen rights, the police force's effective operation is crucial[25].

2. Police Organisation Under Central Government

The federal government of India's police force is made up of a number of specialised units that are in charge of upholding the nation's internal security as well as law and order. To guarantee efficient law enforcement throughout the nation, these forces collaborate with the state police forces.

One of the most significant specialised forces under the central government is the Central Reserve Police Force (CRPF). It is mainly used in regions where there are insurgencies and left-wing extremism. The CRPF is in charge of upholding the rule of law, quelling riots, and battling terrorism.

Another specialised unit under the central government is the Border Security unit (BSF). It is in charge of guarding Bangladesh's and Pakistan's borders with India. Along with other internal security responsibilities, the BSF is also active in anti-smuggling operations.

Various industrial facilities, governmental structures, and airports across the nation must all have security provided by the Central Industrial Security Force (CISF). The CISF is also in charge of protecting VIPs and performing anti-sabotage inspections.

---

24   Chaturvedi, S.K., Role of Police in Criminal Justice System, B.R. Publishing Corporation, Delhi, 1996.
25   Chaturvedi, S.K., Rural Policing In India, B.R. Publishing Corporation, Delhi, 1988.

Operations against terrorism are carried out by the National Security Guard (NSG), a specialised force. In high-risk circumstances like hostage rescue, hijackings, and terrorist assaults, the NSG is prepared to respond.

The federal Bureau of Investigation (CBI), another department of the federal government, is in charge of looking into cases of corruption, economic crimes, and big crimes that have local, national, or worldwide repercussions.

Overall, the central government's police force is essential to the country's ability to uphold law and order and internal security. To ensure efficient law enforcement and the preservation of people' rights, these specialised forces collaborate with the state police forces.

3. Police Commissioners

In cities with a population of more than a million, law and order are administered by police commissioners, senior members of the Indian police force. The British colonial authority originally implemented the police commissioner system in India in 1861, and it is still in use in a number of Indian cities today.

The entire management of peace and order in their individual cities is the responsibility of the police commissioners, who are chosen by the state government. They are in charge of upholding law and order, stopping and investigating crime, and making sure that citizens are safe and secure.

The management of police at the zonal and sub-zonal levels is the responsibility of a number of individuals, including Joint Commissioners of Police (JCP), Deputy Commissioners of Police (DCP), and Assistant Commissioners of Police (ACP)[26].

Maintaining law and order at big events like festivals, processions, and elections is just one of the crucial duties of police commissioners. Additionally, they are in charge of conducting investigations into crimes and prosecuting perpetrators.

---

[26] Deb, R., Principles of Criminology, Criminal Law and Investigation, S.C. Sarkar and Sons, Calcutta, 1958.

To ensure efficient law enforcement and the efficient operation of city services, police commissioners collaborate closely with other governmental entities like the Municipal Corporation, Fire Department, and Traffic Police[27].

In general, the police organisation in India is significant because of the police commissioner system.

It aids in ensuring efficient law enforcement and the preservation of peace and order in densely populated cities. Greater coordination between different police units and other governmental organisations is made possible by the system, which is crucial for the effective operation of the police forces in these cities[28].

[27] Role of Police in Criminal Justice System. - S.K. Chaturvedi
[28] R. Deb, Criminal Justice, [1st Edition, 1998], the Law Book Company Pvt. Limited, Allahabad, P. 13 5.

CHAPTER 3

ROLE OF POLICE IN INDIA: WITH SPECIAL REFERENCE TO PRESENT CRIMINAL JUSTICE SYSTEM

1: Criminal Justice System & its Process

The federal republic of India is made up of 28 states and 7 union territories. 1 The 'Police' are a State affair, according to the Indian Constitution. 2 This guarantees that they fall under local governments' jurisdiction. Each state and union territory has its own law enforcement agency, and the structure and functioning of police officers are governed by state laws and legislation. The union government has also created central law enforcement agencies for specialised duties. The total number of state/union territory police departments in the nation as of 1.1.2002 was 14,49,761. The total strength of the central armed officers organisations was 5,28,370[29]. If properly utilised, this enormous pool of talented workers, which is thought to number over 2 million, might be a powerful force for social improvement in the neighbourhood.

Accountability for them is inextricably tied to the type of oversight and supervision exerted over them. This chapter examines police oversight in India in four sections. The first section explains the fundamental characteristics of the British-established police structure in this nation and demonstrates how the concept of holding the authorities responsible to someone outside the state did not work into the imperial form of policing adopted in this nation[30].

The second section claims that, while post-Independent India saw significant reforms on a variety of grounds the police framework in terms of its fundamental framework, mechanisms of operation, and lack of democratic oversight, stayed mostly intact. Additionally, it addresses the changes that culminated in the tightening of administrative oversight over the policing, resulting in an increase in police brutality and abuse of authority. The third section addresses the importance of holding police officers responsible, mostly in the form of public lawsuits against police officers, and the processes in place to maintain transparency, both inside and beyond the force. The closing section

---

[29]   S.P. Srinivasan (1987). "Criminal Justice Administration in India; Issue and Perspective," International Journal of Criminology, Vol. 15, P. 99.

[30]   Torture, Rape & Death in Custody, Amnesty International India, 1992, Amnesty Interactional Publications, [1st Edition], Easton Street London. P. 76.

summarizes the debate and argues that criminal justice reform is both necessary and essential.

5.2. The Police System - A Colonial Legacy

The Police Act of 1861 established the Police as an organized agency in this land. This law was enacted in response to the 1857 Indian Sepoy Mutiny[31], in which Indian soldiers in the colonial army rose up against their British officers. The rebellion eventually morphed into a revolt against British rule in India. While the rebellion was quickly and effectively put down, it prompted the British to take several measures to strengthen their authority in India, including the creation of an oppressive police department to assist the colonial administration

Section 3 of the 1861 Police Act vests state legislatures with the authority to supervise4 state police forces. The same Act established a dual management structure at the district stage

It placed police powers under the authority of District Superintendents of Police but accountable to the District Judges' "*basic supervision and guidance.*" This was undertaken intentionally as the District Magistrate's position as the district's chief officer was deemed critical to the continuation of British rule in India.

The British set up the system so that they would hold high positions within the army and reserve junior positions for "indigenous people." The lowest echelons of the service are referred to as "substandard policemen" in Section 7 of the 1861 Police Act. The aristocratic prejudice continued even after high jobs were eventually Indianized. The selection of candidates for senior posts has frequently been influenced significantly by family background. They understood that a system based on the feudal customs prevalent in Indian culture would be effective in ensuring that the command and file of the department remained obedient, subordinate, and accountable to their superiors within the organisations or agencies. This led to the development of a management philosophy that emphasised mistrust in the organization's

For instance, according to Section 162 of the Criminal Procedure Code, the testimony of a witness investigated by the policemen during an arrest is not to be certified by the

---

[31]   David, Saul. The Indian Mutiny: 1857. Penguin UK, 2003.

witnesses and cannot be utilized during prosecution for any reason other than to refute the witnesses if he contradicts it.

Likewise, Section 25 of the Indian Evidence Act, 1872[32] provides that police officer-recorded admissions are inadmissible in proof. The police force was institutionalized in a militaristic and bureaucratic fashion. There was a strong focus on maintaining a regimented form of conduct which required the lower levels to follow instructions willingly. The scheme did not mandate officers to wear tactical hats when doing their tasks. They were not, in particular, needed to have any.[33]

It makes sense that the 1861 Act struggled to establish a nationwide police force that was efficient, knowledgeable, and accountable. The colonial rulers realised this. For instance, Sir A.H.L. Fraser's Indian Police Commission, which was established in July 1902, came to the following conclusion: "The policing department is very far from productive; it is inefficient in terms of recruitment and organisation; it is inadequately monitored; it is widely perceived as unethical and authoritarian; and it has completely struggled to earn the public's trust and teamwork."[34].

5.3. Post Independence Developments

Despite changes brought about by independence, the organisation of the police force mainly remained unchanged. The 1861 Police Act also applied to it. Its managerial philosophy, belief system, and cultural foundation have remained stable. Politicians and policymakers still have the power to monitor and control the officers. They were a police force that was friendly to the ruling class and kept a great distance from the populace. Despite the country having been independent for nearly 55 years, neither the federal nor state legislatures have used this time to replace the 1861 Police Act with a more up-to-date statute that adheres to current governance principles. It's not as if no new laws had recently been passed. Since Freedom, the majority of state legislatures have passed new legislation defining how their police enforcement agencies must operate.

For example, the Bombay Police Act of 1951[35] governs the police forces in Maharashtra and Gujarat, the *Kerala Police Act of 1960*[36] governs the police forces in Kerala, the

---

[32] Stephen, James Fitzjames. The Indian Evidence Act (I. of 1872): with an introduction on the principles of judicial evidence. Macmillan and Company, 1872.
[33] Report of the Indian Police Commission, 1902-03: 150.
[34] Report of the Indian Police Commission, 1902-03: 150).

Karnataka Police Act of 1963[37] governs the police forces in Karnataka, and the Delhi Police Act of 1978[38] governs the police forces in Delhi. In 2001, the Madhya Pradesh government introduced a new Police Bill. Additionally, several state authorities have enacted special laws to control the operation of their State Armed Police Forces.

Investigations into police matters in India by nearly all State Police Commissions, the National Police Committee, and other legal professionals yielded unambiguous evidence of politicians misusing police officers for modest personal advantage. This was particularly clear when there were emergencies. (1975 — 1977)[39], during which the police perpetrated widespread massacres. The blatant way in which the policemen were abused during this time caused the central government that took control after the *The Shah Commission*[40] uncovered substantial proof that certain law enforcement officials acted as if they were not responsible to any elected authorities during the Emergencies phase The Shah Commission[41][42] advised the state in its study that "employing the policemen for the benefit of some political group is a sure way to undermine the rule of law," and urged the centralized governments to take steps to protect the policemen from unconstitutional political and administrative influence.

As a result, the Indian governments established the *National Police Commission*[104] (NPC). The NPC was tasked with conducting a thorough study of the law enforcement, taking into account the far-stretching reforms that occurred in the nation after the passage of the Indian Police Act in 1861, the recommendation of the last Police Commission in 1902,[43] and, in particular, the modifications made following Freedom. Protecting police officers from unconstitutional political and institutional interference was the subject of several notable initiatives, including the following:

---

35   Noorani, A. G. "The Constitution and Censorship of Plays." (2008): 31-33.
36   Chatterjee, N. C. "Report of the Kerala Police Reorganisation Committee." (1960).
37   MUKHERJEE, TUMPA. "CHAPTER TWELVE POLICING IN INDIA: CONTEMPORARY ISSUES AND INTROSPECTIONS TUMPA MUKHERJEE." International Perspectives on Crime and Justice (2009): 271.
38   Kumar, N. Origin of Delhi Police-A Geographical Study. Journal Global Values, 8(2).
39   Atre, S., & Ananth, K. (2020). RIGHTS OF THE PEOPLE AND NATIONAL EMERGENCY (1975-77): A CRITICAL ANALYSIS OF A DEBATABLE ERA OF INDIAN POLITICS. International Journal of Management (IJM), 11(11).
40   Shah Commission. Interim report-II. Govt. of India: New Delhi, 1978.
41   Ibid 104 Verma, Arvind. "National Police Commission in India: An analysis of the policy failures." The Police Journal
42   3 (1998): 226-244.
43   Dr.Deepa Singh, Human Rights and Police Predicament 59(The Bright Law House Delhi, 2002).

The creation of an Advisory Council in each jurisdiction to ensure that the state conducts oversight of the police in a transparent and lawful manner;

- Establishing a system for appointing the appropriate personnel to lead state police departments;

- Establishing a set standard period for these personnel to mitigate their vulnerability;

- Modifying laws to render unlawful assignments of policemen made without authorization meaningless; and

- Repealing the 1861 Police Act and enacting a new one. None of the NPC's above guidelines has been adopted.

The entrenched establishment was disturbed by these comments because they feared losing control of an institution that they have long abused. Additionally, politicians and bureaucrats provided a compelling motivation to keep control and direction over the law enforcement organisation and to uphold the status quo.

Failure of the criminal Justice system

Not only are the officers unpopular, but the majority of the criminal justice system's institutions as a whole are as well. The number of crimes has grown. For instance, from 6.25 lakhs in 1951 to 17.7 lakhs in 2000, there were reported overall cognizable criminal offences under the Indian Penal Code (IPC).[44] In 2000, there were over 51.6 lakh crimes that could be considered cognizable, including 33.9 lakh offences that were reported in violation of regional and specialised laws. 15 The public always accuses the police if there is a rise in drug activity or a particularly heinous crime is committed. It has become customary to attribute any increase in violence to the police.

This mindset is reinforced by the policeman's response to outside examination. Either they highlight low crime rates or they bemoan the inadequate staffing and resources at their disposal. Both scenarios include questionable crime rates. The cops are frequently criticised for not appropriately documenting violence. Contrary to popular assumption,

---

[44] Dreze, J., & Khera, R. (2000). Crime, gender, and society in India: Insights from homicide data. Population and development review, 26(2), 335-352.

criminal activity is often hidden or kept under wraps. Because crime is used to gauge police success, this is one of the main causes. This, the NPC asserts, allows "police to use dubious means of documenting and monitoring violence, even stooping to criminal activities."[45]

Conviction rates have fallen precipitously. Although the prosecution rate for IPC offenses was 62 percent in 1971, it had decreased to about 36% by 2000. 18 Justice is both withheld and postponed. The courts are clogged with massive backlogs of pending litigation. As per the Parliamentary Standing Committees on Home Affairs' 61st survey, 25 million lawsuits were facing prosecution in the nation's various courts. 19 Because a vast number of people are able to flee after committing offences and punishment is not doled out to offenders or prosecutions go on over an undetermined period of years in trials, it erodes the public's trust and belief in the program's efficacy.

In areas where there is a high level of crime or violence, it seems to be much harder to hold police officers accountable for their mistakes. Over the past few years, there has been a lot of extremist activity in many counties, including Punjab and J&K. In such regions, terror is rampant, and locals are powerless to help or aid security personnel.

The work of the courts is hampered, and the charges brought by the authorities against terrorists in court are not decided. In such circumstances, the government invariably uses the escalating risk of crime and hostilities to arm itself with authoritarian forces. It passes 'dark' legislation that strengthens the power of the police and restricts the rights of the populace. The police frequently violate civil rights and have practically total discretion[46].

Arbitrary searches, incommunicado incarceration, Disproportionate use of force, disappearances, inhumane treatment of prisoners, and extrajudicial executions are frequently cited as examples of crimes against police officers in these areas. Legal actions against intelligence operatives are typically disregarded by the government on the grounds that doing so would demoralise police officers and weaken their resolve to crush organised crime with a heavy hand. This has happened on several occasions. For instance, during the earliest stages of the unrest in Punjab, the State and, to a lesser extent, the populace

45   Ibid 109 Bayley, David H. "The police and political change in comparative perspective." Law & society review 6.1 (1971): 91-112.
46   http://www.groundreport.com/Business/Human-Right-organisations-often-accusedBengal-police, visited on 4-7-2010. 190.2004-2005 Annual Report of NHRC.

tolerated egregious violations of human rights. However, as peace and normalcy restored, civil community organisations played a crucial role in pushing for police officers to remain accountable for any injustices committed in the years before.

The Times of India reported in September 1997 [47]that 123 police officers were standing prosecution for using abusive tactics against militants, citing statistics from the Union Home Ministry. Additionally, individuals and civil rights organisations had filed 2,555 grievances against Punjab officers.

On the other side, the general consensus is that in most cases, the government stands up for police officers. Generally, where the state demands the policeman to address critical or important law and order issues of political importance, such as extremism, police atrocities receive tacit or overt sanction, if not reinforcement and protection, from the state. Occasionally, assurances of immunity are provided in anticipation. An illustration can be contained in the reply delivered on April 30, 1998, by Mr. Kalyan Singh[48], the then-chief minister of Uttar Pradesh (UP). While briefing state law enforcement officials at a peace and justice briefing in Lucknow, the Chief Minister stated: "I expect success outcomes." I want you to swear that you will bring in a dhamaka (eruption) in the province. While convicted felons may be

apprehended in interactions, do so. If you kill one individual who has killed ten others, you will be praised. And I'm here to safeguard you."[49]

Law enforcement officials are given more freedom to abuse their powers or to be complacent when the promise of impunity is made by the highest echelons of the government. They are well aware that they cannot be held accountable for their acts of gross negligence or wrongdoing. This was especially evident during the community conflict that erupted in Gujarat between February and April 2002[50].

The Authorities were unable to quell the protests, which lasted more than three months and resulted in significant loss of life and property for black local residents. There is

[47] Verma, Arvind. "Taking justice outside the courts: Judicial activism in India." The Howard Journal of Criminal Justice 40.2 (2001): 148-165.
[48] Ojha, Suman. "CONFIDENCE MOTION: An emerging trend in the Uttar Pradesh legislature." The Indian Journal of Political Science (2010): 525-533.
[49] Rakesh Mohan, Police and Human Rights6 (Swastika Publications, N.Delhi, 2013).
[50] Shani, Ornit. Communalism, caste and Hindu nationalism: The violence in Gujarat. Cambridge University Press, 2007.

substantial proof that the officers were involved in many incidents and certainly didn't come to the survivors' help. According to sources, the state legislature was prejudiced against the minority group and did not want the authorities to successfully suppress the disturbances.

The risk of the public turning a blind eye to the police's use of unethical tactics is especially pronounced in places where militants, rebels, or perpetrators are representatives of marginalized groups and their violent acts are directed toward representatives of the dominant population. In some situations, the public does not take seriously police brutality against alleged criminals or their allies.

There is a clause of the constitution that allows the government to grant impunity for alleged wrongdoing. This clause is included in Section 197 of the Criminal Procedure Code, which prohibits prosecution of a civil officer without the approval of the competent authority for actions committed "whether serving or claiming to be in the performance of his professional functions." The object of this section of law is to prevent law enforcement officials from being demoralized and dissuaded from fulfilling their duties by the filing of unfounded and scurrilous grievances.

However, it is a reality that this clause of the statute has been exploited to exclude law enforcement personnel from prosecution except in the most egregious instances of wrongdoing. This occurs as a result of a nexus between lawmakers, administrators, and law enforcement officials which purposefully prevents or refuses prosecution penalties. The National Police Committee's suggestions to revoke police forces' safety under Section 197 of the CrPC. 1973 were not approved.

There is clear proof in India of an increase in police deviant behavior. Indian media often document on instances of police abuse, theft, and other crimes perpetrated by policemen in various parts of the world. According to the National Human Rights Commission's records[51], the numbers of lawsuits filed about 'fatalities in police detention' rose from 136 in 1995-96 to 177 in 1999-2000.

---

[51] Channabasavanna, S. M., and Pratima Murthy. "The National human rights Commission report 1999: a defining moment." Mental health: An Indian perspective 1946–2003 (2004): 108-112.

The National Human Rights Commission (NHRC[52]) receives the bulk of lawsuits against police officers. Also government reports show that police stations collect a large volume of citizen allegations against officers. According to a survey by the

National Crime Records Bureau (NCRB), a Government of India agency, the public lodged 1,23,523 allegations against the cops in 1997.

The proposed procedures for holding police officers accountable for their conduct may be classified narrowly into two categories:

1. **Internal Accountability Mechanisms.**

2. **External Accountability Mechanisms**

External accountability procedures for particular policemen are outlined in the 1861 Police Act, state police acts, and laws found in particular security guides. The Police Act of 1861[53] empowers professional policemen with the position of Superintendent of Police and above to terminate, detain, or demote any policeman of subordinate levels they believe is negligent or unable to perform his or her duties.

Additionally, they are authorized to enforce all or more of the following penalties:

(a)   A penalty not to surpass one month's salary,

(b)   Imprisonment to quarters not to surpass 15 days,

(c)   Denial of good behaviour payment, and

(d)   Dismissal from any position of recognition or unique indemnification.

Additionally, the 1861 Police Act currently lists offenses for which a policeman can be reprimanded:

(i)   Wilful violation or negligence of any law, legislation, or legal command;

(ii)   Removal from office tasks or absence without authorization or appropriate cause

---

[52]   Ibid
[53]   Supra

(iii) Participating in any occupation apart from his policing duties without authorization;

(iv) Cowardliness; and

(v) Inducing any ugliness.[54]

The punishment for these offenses is a fine of up to three months' salary, up to three months' detention, or a mixture of the two. The laws categorize penalties as 'major' or 'minor'. Though state laws vary, suspension, elimination, decrease of rank or salary, and duty revocation are all considered' major penalties'. They cannot be placed on any police officer without a departmental investigation. Only after the investigation establishes the allegations against the convicted police officer will a significant punishment be levied. Censure and disciplinary action are examples of minor penalties. They can be levied in the absence of any individual departments' legal measures.

Courts are a critical external tool for maintaining police transparency. Although higher courts can hear writ appeals and public interest cases, lower courts can hear felony trials. The higher courts have issued a number of significant judgments, establishing protections or protocols to monitor law enforcement throughout detention, questioning, and other phases of interrogation, ordering the state to compensate victims of prevalence of violence, criticizing the police for displaying prejudice in the treatment of religious and caste disputes, and imposing strenuous sentences.

On December 18, 1997, the Supreme Court issued a historic decision directed at shielding the Central Bureau of Investigation and the Directorate of Enforcement from external interference[55], allowing them to operate effectively and transparently in the service of the rule of law.

Additionally, the Judgment ruled null and invalid the Single Directive, which mandated the CBI to obtain approval from the government prior to conducting any inquiry or examination against senior executives with the status of Joint Secretary or higher. For more than five years, the state eventually passed legislation reinstating the Single

---

[54]   Rakesh Mohan, Police and Human Rights3(Swastika Publications, N.Delhi, 2013).
[55]   Mikos, Robert A. "A critical appraisal of the Department of Justice's new approach to medical marijuana." Stan. L. & Pol'y Rev. 22 (2011): 633.

Directive. One significant issue is the lack of any process for monitoring the execution of these judgments and remanding the insolvent state or other party to the courts.[56]

5.8 Non-government organizations

NGO practices pertaining to the police are narrowly classified into two categories: those dealing with police officer-initiated human rights abuses and those associated with police organization changes.

The former category of actions entails exposing police brutality and pressuring the authorities to enact measures against the officers. Typically, the police or government's response to NGO accusations is rejection. The government is traditionally averse to disclosing police misuse of authority for fear of it being held against them by the opposition. However, where credible proof of human rights abuses is accompanied by indisputable facts, the state is compelled to respond. However, reporting human rights abuses perpetrated by police officers presents a significant problem for NGOs.

When evidence of rights violations is supported by undeniable facts, the state must act. Reporting police abuses of human rights, however, is a substantial challenge for NGOs.

The job is difficult due to the intimidating nature of the position as well as a lack of experience. The NGO lacks the expertise necessary to effectively advocate for workable alternatives to present police modernization programmes or to suggest systemic intervention. For instance, the police neglected to document the complaints of many victims who belonged to minority ethnic groups during Gujarat's sectarian persecution. Many plaintiffs were denied access to compensation and justice in court.

Investigation, arrest, trial, and punishment are only a few of the phases of India's multi-stage criminal justice system. The procedure starts when a crime is reported to the police, who then look into it and gather evidence.

The suspect will be taken into custody and brought before a magistrate if the police suspect that a crime has been committed. The magistrate next determines whether to release the suspect on bail or keep him or her in custody.

---

[56] Dalbir Bharti, Police and People, Role and Responsibilities68(APH Publishing House, New Delhi, 2006).

After the defendant is placed on remand, the police finish their inquiry and submit a charge sheet to the court. Information about the crime, the evidence gathered, and the identities of the witnesses are all included on the charge sheet.

The criminal justice system in India is guided by several laws, including the Indian Penal Code (IPC), the Criminal Procedure Code (CrPC), and the Indian Evidence Act. These laws are designed to ensure justice is served and the rights of both the accused and the victims are protected.

The accused is provided with a lawyer and witnesses are called to testify. If the court finds the accused guilty, they are sentenced, which can range from a fine to life imprisonment or the death penalty.

The criminal justice system in India has been criticized for its slow pace, high rates of acquittal, and outdated laws. However, efforts are being made to improve the system by introducing new laws, increasing the use of technology, and improving the training of police and judicial officers. The police have an important responsibility in the investigation and prosecution of crimes, and their actions can have a significant impact on the outcome of a case..

The Supreme Court observed that, "it should be an acceptable practice of authority, consistent with maintaining a rational and equitable prosecutorial process that judges submit a particular conclusion in these instances, after documenting explanations for willful gross negligence, deliberately deficient inquiry, and willful actions of negligence and conduct bigoted to the government's case and in violation of professed privilege."

Additionally, the judiciary will be entirely reasonable in ordering the administrative power to enforce reasonable compliance or other steps in compliance with the rules, regardless of whether the agent, specialist, or worker eyewitness is still employed or has resigned."

In view of the preceding decision, it is evident that misconduct would not have to have a detrimental impact on the criminal trial in order to establish the policeman's innocence. If there is a risk of detrimental impact or if a court argument fails as a consequence of the investigative cop's negligence, there is a valid reason to bring suit against the officers involved.

A police agent is required to behave faithfully and solely within the bounds of the rule. Any violation of ethical ethics that occurs during the process of the inquiry must be taken seriously. It is self-evident that in order to determine if the police are abusing their policing authority, only their actions of commission or omission must be considered.

2: Role of Police Towards Criminal Justice System.

In India's criminal justice system, the police are essential. They are in charge of upholding the law, preventing crime, and maintaining safety for everyone. The investigation and prosecution of crimes are major tasks for the police.

Conducting unbiased and thorough investigations into criminal cases is one of the police's main responsibilities within the criminal justice system. This entails gathering proof, speaking with witnesses, and locating suspects. The police must make sure that the investigation is carried out legally and that the evidence gathered is admissible in court.

The police are essential in both the arrest and detention of suspects. They must make sure that the rights of the accused are upheld and that they get fair and compassionate treatment while they are detained. When conducting arrests and holding individuals in custody, the police are required to adhere to the steps provided in the Criminal Procedure Code (CrPC).

The police are essential in preserving the public's safety and security in addition to conducting investigations and making arrests. They are in charge of upholding law and order, stopping and dealing with acts of violence and terrorism, and controlling public gatherings and protests.

The police are responsible for providing security and protection to key individuals and institutions, such as politicians, judges, and government buildings. They have a crucial role in the criminal justice system in India, maintaining law and order, investigating crimes, and ensuring the safety and security of the public. To perform their role effectively, the police must be trained, equipped, and supported to carry out their duties professionally, fairly, and impartially.

Section 154 of the Criminal Procedure Code. According to this Section, the police officer is required to record all information that is given to him or her, whether it is verbally or in writing. The person who has been told of the offense's commission should also get the written information. The submitted information must then be appended to the book of records. Any person may convey such information straight to the Superintendent of Police if they are upset that the officer in charge is refusing to take it. Making entries in the investigation's log book is the first step.

The purpose of this Section is to make the District Superintendent of Police, who is in charge of maintaining safety and peace, aware of the commission of the offence, as well as the Magistrate who has jurisdiction over that specific region. Another goal is to familiarise the judicial officers—who will ultimately hear the case—with the relevant facts and evidence. This Section also protects the accused from future modifications and additions, which the prosecution may occasionally make. The filing of the FIR should be regarded as a prerequisite to opening the inquiry, as decided in the case of *Ashok Kumar Todi* v. *Kishwar Jahan (2011)*.

A First Information Report (FIR) is the name for the information provided to the police or official in charge of the police station regarding the commission of a cognizable offence. It is the details provided to the police regarding the commission of the crime. This is the starting point for a case investigation. The police officer's information is reduced to writing and produces a First Information Report. FIR is recorded under Section 154 of the CrPC even though it is not specified anywhere in the law. In circumstances of a cognizable offence, a FIR signifies the start of the inquiry.

If the information pertains to the commission of the cognizable offence, the police officer in charge is required to document the information given to him. According to the ruling in the 2013 case *State of U.P.* v. *Mukesh*, a FIR is a notification that an incident has occurred. It should be highlighted that only the most important information should be recorded in the regular journal. Furthermore, not all facts should be sourced to this material.

The police station that has authority over the location of the occurrence is typically where the FIR is filed. This is not a necessary clause, and if the situation calls for it, it can also be placed elsewhere. Simply put, the FIR may still be filed at that police station even if the police do not have territorial jurisdiction over the crime scene. If the police dispute filing a FIR, this relates to improper behaviour by the police and is viewed as a breach of duty. The FIR that is filed, no matter where the crime occurred, is known as a "Zero FIR." The tragic incident that resulted in the "zero" FIR concept being added to the criminal law after the unfortunate incident of the Nirbhaya gang rape case, on the recommendation of Justice Verma's Committee.

When filing a zero FIR, the police first file the complaint and then transfer it to the police station that has authority over the incident's location.

The concept of zero FIR is intended to encourage prompt FIR filing in order to prevent any unnecessary delays. No matter where the incident occurred, the police have a responsibility to file a FIR in such cases.

When the police begin an investigation based on verbal information provided by an informant and then reduce that information to writing, that information must be treated as a statement under Section 161 of the Criminal Procedure Code rather than a FIR. The second piece of information cannot ever be considered a formal police report.

It should be emphasised that the FIR does not need that it contain real-time details concerning the commission of the offence. It is possible to treat even a straightforward phone message that the police received as a FIR and to note it in the station diary. In the case of *Tapinder Singh* v. *State of Punjab (1970)*, it was decided that telephonic messages containing anonymous information that failed to identify a criminal conduct could not be considered as formal police reports (FIRs). The station's information does not automatically have the meaning of a FIR just because it was received there first in time. To help a legal proceeding, the written information must at the very least mention the penal laws.

The investigation of a criminal case is led by the police in the greatest measure. As required by Indian law, police must look into the cognizable matter and discover the facts. As was previously noted, only cognizable cases are subject to police investigation; otherwise, prior approval from the Magistrate is required. When conducting an investigation in a criminal case, police are responsible for carrying out a variety of tasks, including making arrests, dispersing unauthorised gatherings, adopting proactive measures, and many more. A typical step before a trial is the police investigation of offences that are punishable by law.

In accordance with Section 156 of the CrPC, the police are authorised to investigate cases that are cognizable. According to the Section, any official in charge of a police station may begin an investigation into a case involving a cognizable offence without the Magistrate's consent. The police officer cannot be questioned at any point during the ongoing trial on the grounds that he lacked the authority to conduct an investigation under this Section.

Once an investigation has begun, it won't be over until the police submit a report as required under Section 173 of the Criminal Procedure Code. A cognizable offence may be investigated by the police under Section 156, even without a magistrate's permission. Additionally, under Section 190 of the CrPC, the Magistrate may direct the initiation of an investigation if the police do not do so on their own. A cognizable offence must have occurred for the police to begin the investigation procedure under this Section without a FIR.

It should be remembered that the Magistrate has no authority to halt or direct an investigation that the police are conducting. The Court may decide whether or not to take action after filling up the charge sheet, but the right granted to the police is statutory and cannot be limited by the Court. The Court's role does not, however, start until the charge sheet is submitted. According to Section 156(2) of the CrPC, the police also have the authority to look into offences that are cognizable outside of their territorial jurisdiction.

In *Prabal Dogra* v. *Superintendent of Police, Gwalior and State of M.P. (2018),* it was determined that the High Court could not use its authority under Section 482 of the Criminal Procedure Code to order or direct the police to search for a specific viewpoint or in a specific direction. Additionally, the Court is not permitted to direct the investigation in any way it sees fit. It went on to say that investigation is solely the responsibility of the police, and that responsibility should be treated with respect.

To the contrary, the court ruled in T.T. *Antony* v. *State of Kerala (2001)* that the police should not go beyond their authority. If this occurs, the High Court may, in the interest of justice and in accordance with Section 482 of the CrPC and Articles 226 and 227 of the Indian Constitution, order the police to cease their inquiry in order to stop the misuse of their authority.

It is a well-established notion that even the accused has a right to a fair investigation, thus the police ensure justice by conducting such an investigation. An important step in determining whether a crime was committed honestly and accurately is to launch an investigation. Any obstruction of the legal process must be avoided since doing so will amount to a miscarriage of justice. In general, police are also permitted to begin an investigation prior to filing a FIR; but, in situations involving unnatural deaths, filing a FIR is required.

3: Legal functioning of Police

The legal functioning of the police in India is governed by several laws and regulations. The primary law is the Indian Police Act, 1861, which outlines the organization and functioning of the police force and provides guidelines for the conduct of police officers. The Criminal Procedure Code (CrPC) outlines the procedures that the police must follow in investigating and prosecuting criminal cases and provides guidelines for the arrest, detention, and interrogation of suspects. The Constitution of India guarantees several fundamental rights, including the right to life, liberty, and equality before the law. The police must ensure that these rights are protected and respected in carrying out their duties.

Several actions have been made in recent years to guarantee that the legal operation of the police complies with human rights norms. One of these is the creation of oversight agencies that are tasked with keeping an eye on police behaviour and looking into allegations of human rights abuses, such as the National Human Rights Commission and the State Human Rights Commissions.

Several laws and regulations, which are intended to ensure that the police's acts are lawful, moral, and compliant with human rights principles, serve as a general framework for the legal functioning of the police in India. To perform their tasks competently, fairly, and impartially while upholding the rule of law and everyone's rights, the police must have the necessary training, tools, and resources.

a) Patrolling and Surveillance

In India, patrolling and surveillance are crucial police duties. Patrolling and surveillance are essential instruments for preventing and detecting criminal activity. The police are responsible for upholding law and order in their area of responsibility.

Police personnel move routinely and methodically around their area on foot, bicycles, or in cars as part of patrolling. In order to prevent criminal activity, respond rapidly to emergencies, and obtain information about prospective criminal activity, patrols are conducted.

Monitoring the actions of people or organisations who are allegedly participating in illegal activity constitutes surveillance. Physical, electronic, and undercover investigations are just a few of the surveillance techniques the police may employ.

The legal framework governing the police's patrolling and surveillance activities is based on several laws and regulations. The Indian Police Act, 1861 provides the legal basis for the activities, while the Code of Criminal Procedure (CrPC) outlines the powers of the police in conducting surveillance and gathering evidence.

To ensure that the activities are carried out legally and ethically, several measures have been taken in recent years, such as the establishment of oversight mechanisms such as the National Human Rights Commission and the State Human Rights Commissions. These mechanisms are responsible for monitoring police conduct and investigating complaints of human rights violations.

In India, patrolling and surveillance are crucial police duties, but they must be carried out in accordance with the law and with regard for basic human rights. The police must make sure that their actions are reasonable, required, and done with the highest regard for the law and everyone's rights.

b) Preventive Functions:

The legitimate operation of the police in India must include preventive actions. The police are in charge of preventing crimes and upholding law and order within their area of responsibility. Police preventive operations are designed to lessen the possibility that crimes will be committed and to maintain public safety.

The police can take a number of preventive actions, such as routine monitoring and observation, the construction of checkpoints and barricades, as well as searches and raids. In addition, they have the authority to hold people who are thought to be involved in criminal activity and to enforce the law.

The legal basis for the preventive functions of the police in India is provided by several laws and regulations, including the Indian Penal Code, the Code of Criminal Procedure, and the Police Act of 1861. To ensure that the preventive functions of the police are carried out legally and ethically, several measures have been taken in recent years. These include the establishment of oversight mechanisms, such as the National Human Rights Commission and the State Human Rights Commissions, which are responsible for monitoring police conduct and investigating complaints of human rights violations. Overall, preventive functions are a critical aspect of the legal functioning of the police in India, and must be carried out in compliance with the law and respect for human rights principles.

c) Investigation by Police

The legal operation of the police in India must also include investigation. The police are in charge of conducting a comprehensive investigation after a crime has been reported in order to find the offender, gather proof, and create a case for prosecution.

In India, the investigative process is governed by the Code of Criminal Procedure (CrPC). The police are authorised by the CrPC to look into any offence that is cognizable without obtaining a warrant. If they have good reason to think that the person has committed an infraction, they may also detain them without a warrant.

The police must adhere to a set of guidelines while conducting the investigation in order for the evidence they gather to be used as evidence in court. These steps entail obtaining tangible evidence, conducting searches and seizures, and recording the statements of witnesses and suspects.

Numerous changes have been made in recent years with the goal of raising the standard of police investigations in India. In order to guarantee that the police conduct investigations in a fair, impartial, and effective manner, the Supreme Court of India has established instructions. The procedures include advice on gathering and keeping records of evidence, handling suspects, and taking statements.

Despite these attempts, there have been a number of complaints about the Indian investigative procedure. Police brutality, forced confessions, and evidence fabrication have all allegedly occurred. Due to these problems, the public no longer has faith in the police and the criminal justice system.

There have been proposals for more reforms to enhance the inquiry process in India to solve these problems. These changes include the creation of impartial investigation agencies and the application of technology to increase the effectiveness and precision of inquiries.

d) Interrogation of Offenders

A crucial component of the Indian police's ability to operate legally is the interrogation of criminals. It is the process of interrogating a suspect in order to gather evidence that will be utilised to support a case against them. The Code of Criminal Procedure (CrPC) and other Indian regulations govern the interrogation procedure.

While holding an offender, the police have the right to question them, but they are also subject to strict guidelines. The police are not permitted to force the offender to provide information by means of coercion, torture, or other cruel treatment. The offender's human rights are violated by this, which is prohibited.

During the interrogation, the police must advise the suspect of their right to a lawyer and their right to remain silent. The police are required to give the criminal access to legal counsel if they ask for it.

The police must accurately and fairly record the offender's remarks made during the interrogation. The CrPC mandates that all interrogations be documented, whether orally or in writing, and that the individual providing the statement sign the documentation.

The use of torture and coercion during police interrogations in India has raised concerns. Numerous allegations of police violence and torture during interrogations have been made to the National Human Rights Commission (NHRC). To stop such actions and guarantee that offenders are treated with respect and dignity, the NHRC has provided police with guidelines.

To aid in interrogations, efforts have been made in recent years to include contemporary procedures like polygraph exams and narco-analysis. These methods, nevertheless, have drawn criticism for allegedly infringing the human rights of the criminal. These methods must be used with the court's approval and are subject to legal restrictions.

e) Control of juvenile delinquency

Controlling adolescent delinquency is a part of the police's legal duties in India. When minors act in a way that breaks the law, this is referred to as juvenile delinquency. The Juvenile Justice (Care and Protection of Children) Act, 2015 governs the juvenile delinquency of children in India.

According to the Act, it is the responsibility of the police to make sure that children who are in trouble with the law are treated in a way that is in their best interests and that their rights are upheld. The Act outlines specific processes for handling young offenders.

The minor Justice Board (JJB) must be immediately notified by the police when a minor is accused of a crime. The JJB is a specialised court that handles situations involving kids who have run afoul of the law. The JJB must decide whether the minor should be released on bond or sent to a special home.

The police must also take action to guarantee the minor's security and welfare while they are detained. This entails giving children food, clothing, and medical attention, as well as making sure they get no physical or mental abuse.

The police are required to conduct investigations in a way that is sensitive to the needs of the juvenile. This includes questioning the juvenile in the presence of a parent or guardian, providing legal aid, and recording statements accurately. In cases where the juvenile is found guilty of an offense, the police must ensure that they receive appropriate rehabilitation and counselling. The Act lays down detailed procedures for the rehabilitation of juvenile offenders, such as vocational training, education, and counselling.

The legal functioning of the police with respect to juvenile delinquency involves ensuring that the rights of the child are protected, that they are treated with dignity and respect, and that they receive appropriate rehabilitation and counselling.

f) Maintain Inquest Register

In India, keeping an inquest register is a crucial legal duty of the police. An inquest is an investigation into the cause of a death, and the aim of an inquest register is to keep track of the specifics of such investigations.

If a person dies in questionable circumstances or if the cause of death is unclear, the police are mandated by the Code of Criminal Procedure (CrPC) to hold an inquest. A police officer with a minimum sub-inspector level oversees the inquest.

The police officer is supposed to examine the deceased person's corpse at the inquest, note any injuries or marks on the body, and document the statements of any witnesses who could have knowledge regarding the circumstances of the death. The police officer must also take any items they discover on or around the body and, if necessary, send them for forensic analysis.

The police officer is obligated to write a report known as the inquest report when the inquest is finished. The specifics of the body's examination, witness testimony, and any other pertinent information must be included in the inquest report. The police officer must sign the report before submitting it to the magistrate in charge.

A record of all police-conducted inquests must be kept by the police officer in the form of an inquest register. The deceased person's name, date and time of death, cause of death, and information about the inquest report must all be included in the registry. In India, it is a crucial legal duty of the police to ensure that investigations into the circumstances of deaths are carried out in a way that is open and accountable.

g) Search and Seizure

In India, search and seizure, which entails searching a person's home or possessions and seizing any potentially damning evidence, is a crucial police role. The police encounter a number of issues and difficulties when performing searches and seizures, though.

The police's inadequate training and ignorance of the laws governing search and seizure is one of their biggest issues. The requisite legal and procedural understanding is frequently lacking among police personnel while performing a search and seizure. This may result in unauthorised or incorrect searches, which may violate someone's privacy and give rise to legal issues.

False or baseless allegations against the police for carrying out unauthorised searches and seizures provide another difficulty. In some instances, people could file fictitious complaints to avoid facing legal consequences or settle personal grudges. This could result in unwarranted harassment of the police and legal issues.

The general public's lack of cooperation during search and seizure operations is another issue the police must deal with. The public frequently opposes police searches of their properties or possessions, and this opposition can be difficult for the police to handle. This can cause the inquiry to drag out and make it harder to gather important evidence.

Inaccessible locations with difficult terrain and unpredictable weather present considerable difficulties for the police in India while conducting searches and seizures.

The public's effective collaboration and assistance, as well as appropriate training and awareness programmes, are all necessary for the police to effectively address these concerns.

 The police require appropriate education and awareness campaigns, as well as efficient public support and cooperation, to handle these issues.

h) To Assist the Prosecutor

In India, the police play a crucial part in the criminal justice system, yet they encounter several obstacles in doing so. These issues include a lack of coordination and communication between the prosecutor's office and the police, fraud and undue influence on the side of the defendants and their supporters, obstacles with gathering and presenting evidence, and issues with dealing with witnesses. Better communication and collaboration between the police and the prosecutor's office, specialised training for police officers, and efficient witness protection and support are all required to solve these issues.

i) Identification etc

In India's criminal justice system, the police play a vital role in the identification of suspects. To effectively carry out this function, the police must overcome a number of obstacles.

The lack of contemporary forensic methods and tools is one of the biggest problems. The identification of suspects may be imprecise and unreliable when obsolete methods and tools are used. Additionally, the lack of qualified workers in the field of forensic science makes the issue worse.

The problem of mistaken identity presents another difficulty. On the basis of mistaken identity, the police may hold and arrest innocent people, which could result in erroneous charges and convictions. This may also lead to a decline in public confidence in law enforcement and the criminal justice system.

In addition, dealing with incidents where the suspect isn't at the crime site or where a group of people committed the crime may offer difficulties for the police. In these situations, the authorities may be forced to rely on eyewitness testimony, which is frequently biased and rife with inaccuracies.

In addition, dealing with situations where the suspect is a serial offender and has altered their appearance or identity may present difficulties for the police. Because of this, it could be challenging for the authorities to locate and capture the suspect.

In India, the police are in charge of apprehending criminals, but they have difficulties like a lack of contemporary forensic methods and tools, mistaken identity, reliance on eyewitness reports, and difficulty with repeat offenders. greater police training and equipment, greater coordination and communication between the various agencies involved in the criminal justice system, and the application of contemporary technology and methodologies are required to meet these difficulties.

j) General Welfare Functions

In addition to their core responsibility for upholding law and order, the police in India are also in charge of carrying out a variety of general welfare duties. To effectively carry out these duties, the police must overcome a number of obstacles.

Lack of enough resources and manpower is one of the main issues. As a result, it could be challenging for the police to carry out tasks like community policing, crime prevention, and public awareness initiatives.

It may be challenging for the police to interact with communities and effectively address their concerns if there is a lack of public confidence and collaboration. The people may also be hostile or unwilling to cooperate with the police, which can make it more difficult for them to uphold the law and offer services for the general welfare of the community.

Additionally, it's possible that the police lack the expertise or resources needed to deal with problems like drug misuse, domestic violence, and other social problems. In addition, there may be difficulties for the police in coordinating and cooperating with other organisations and parties involved in delivering general welfare services, which could result in duplication of effort, inefficiencies, and gaps in service delivery.

The police in India are tasked with a variety of public welfare tasks in addition to upholding law and order, but it can be difficult for them to carry out these duties successfully due to a number of factors.

Adequate funding and manpower, improved police training and skill development, increased public trust and cooperation, and better coordination and collaboration between various agencies and stakeholders involved in providing general welfare services are all necessary to address these issues.

k) Conditional release of accused on Bond

An accused person may be released from detention while awaiting trial through the legal procedure known as conditional release of accused on bond or bail, provided that certain requirements are met, such as the provision of a guarantee or monetary deposit. The cops must overcome a number of obstacles to successfully implement it, though.

One of these difficulties is the problem of phoney or fraudulent sureties, which can make it difficult for the authorities to find the suspects if they skip court. The problem of serial offenders who are repeatedly released on bail presents another difficulty since it might endanger public safety and erode public confidence in the criminal justice system.

The process of releasing suspects on bond or bail[57] can take a long time and require a lot of police resources, which can cause delays in the criminal justice system.

 Enforcing the terms of parole imposed on the accused, such as requiring them to regularly report to a police station or remain inside a specific region, may also provide difficulties. This makes it more challenging to find the guilty and enforce the terms of their release.

4: Problems Faced by the Police

Numerous issues the Indian police must deal with have an affect on how well they can do their duties. The absence of proper staff, education, and equipment is one of the biggest problems facing the police.

This can result in police officers having low morale and being ineffective, and it can also make it challenging to uphold law and order in high-crime regions (Ghosh, 2018)[58].

The prevalence of corruption and wrongdoing inside the police is a problem they also deal with. This may damage the public's confidence in the police and jeopardise their capacity to uphold law and order.

According to a 2019 Transparency International report, the police are the most dishonest government agency in India, with more than half of survey participants admitting to paying bribes to police in the previous year (Transparency International India, 2019)[59].

The police also frequently deal with difficulties brought on by political meddling and pressure, which can result in prejudice in investigations and erroneous arrests.

Police are unwilling to look into crimes involving influential politicians or their friends due to political pressure placed on the force, according to a report by Human Rights Watch (Human Rights Watch, 2016)[60].

The usage of the antiquated Section 377 of the Indian Penal Code, which criminalises consenting same-sex relationships, is only one example of the difficulties that Indian police must contend with due to outmoded laws and practises.

The police may find it challenging to carry out their duties in an efficient, fair, and equitable manner as a result of this uncertainty (Sengupta, 2018)[61].

In general, the issues the Indian police must deal with are complicated and multidimensional, necessitating a variety of changes and interventions.

---

[58] Ghosh, A. (2018). Policing in India: Challenges and Prospects. International Journal of Innovative Research and Development, 7(5), 1-7.
[59] Transparency International India. (2019). India Corruption Survey 2019.
[60] Human Rights Watch. (2016). "These Fellows Must Be Eliminated": Relentless Violence and Impunity in Uttar Pradesh.
[61] Sengupta, S. (2018). Policing consensual sex: Section 377 and the police in India.

To combat corruption and political meddling in the police force, there must be a strong political will, as well as enough resources and training for the police.

TROUBLESHOOT THE POLICE HAVE IN THEIR INVESTIGATION[62]

i)   Every time, the country's police and investigation institutions' overall credibility is questioned. However, I think it is absurd to say that all police officers are dishonest.

ii)   One of the difficulties the police frequently run into while conducting an investigation is their incapacity to continually question an accused person in order to confirm the accuracy of the claims they have made. The police can only learn pertinent information about the crime by thoroughly and persistently questioning the accused. However, police detention and questioning are only permitted for a total of 14 days. Custodial interrogation enables the police to confront the witnesses and the accused and gets information from them that can be used to corroborate other evidence. Therefore, it is necessary to permit police custody and questioning as a matter of right. The 14-day term of police detention does not have to be continuous. Police would really want it to be intermittent since confronting the accused with the information gathered is crucial towards the conclusion of an investigation[63].

iii)   The police frequently point to a lack of adequate investigative resources, hostile witnesses, widespread apathy, and lack of faith in the police as reasons for their inability to bring a criminal to justice. The biggest obstacle to solving crimes is to gather all evidence linking the crime to the criminals who committed it and to ensure its preservation in a tamper-proof state and in a way that is permitted by law[64].

---

[62]   Ibid
[63]   Ibid
[64]   Ibid

CHAPTER 4
THE PROCESS AND PROCEDURE OF INVESTIGATION

1: Introduction

The gathering, examination, and appraisal of evidence relevant to a criminal offence constitute an essential step in the criminal justice system. It is a crucial step in bringing the criminal to justice and guaranteeing just treatment of all parties.

The investigation process is crucial in deciding whether the accused is guilty or innocent, thus it needs to be well planned, carried out, and documented. The systematic and scientific approach of conducting an inquiry to gather evidence, establish facts, and identify the perpetrator of a crime is referred to in this context as the investigative process and procedure.

2: The Process and Procedure of Investigation.

The following steps can be used to roughly split the investigative process and procedure:

- *Information Gathering*: Getting information regarding a crime is the first stage in any inquiry. This can be provided by a number of people, including a victim, a witness, or an anonymous tip. The investigator must ascertain the accuracy of the information and must accurately document it.

- *Planning*: After receiving the facts, the investigator must design their inquiry. This include defining the investigation's parameters, allocating resources, and figuring out how things happened.

- *Examining the Scene:* The investigator must go to the crime scene to gather tangible evidence, such as photos, videos, and sketches. The scene analysis is important since it serves as the basis for the inquiry.

- *Evidence Gathering:* After inspecting the scene, the investigator must gather the tangible proof. This includes traces of evidence including fingerprints, DNA, hair, and fibres. The proof needs to be gathered scientifically and well documented.

- *Interviews and interrogations:* In order to learn more about the crime, the investigator must speak with witnesses and question suspects. To prevent any violations of human rights, attention must be taken during the interview and interrogation procedure.

- *Evidence analysis and evaluation:* After the evidence has been gathered, it needs to be examined and assessed. This includes forensic inspection, lab testing, and a comparison of the evidence with existing samples.

- *Reconstruction:* The investigator needs to retrace the events that happened before and after the incident. This entails looking at the evidence gathered and putting a logical chain of events together utilising it.

- *Report Writing:* The investigator is required to write a report that summarises the results of the inquiry. A description of the evidence gathered, an analysis and evaluation of the evidence, and conclusions should all be included in the report, which must be factual and impartial.

- *Evidence Presentation:* In a criminal trial, the investigator is required to present the evidence. To guarantee that the evidence is admissible in court, it must be presented logically and methodically[65].

In conclusion, the investigation process and procedures are essential to ensuring the impartial administration of justice. To ensure that the evidence gathered is admissible in court and the culprit is brought to justice, the investigation must be carried out with the highest care and precision[66].

---

[65] JAMES VADACKUMCHERY, INDIAN POLICE AND MISCARRIAGE OF JUSTICE, 18, (APH Publishing Corporation, New Delhi, 1997)
[66] RAKESH MOHAN, POLICE AND HUMAN RIGHTS, 2, (Swastika Publications, N. Delhi, 2013).

3: Legal Provisions of CRPC Related to Investigation.

The primary piece of legislation in India that establishes the procedural rules for the investigation of criminal offences is the Code of Criminal Procedure (CRPC). Some of the significant law clauses pertaining to CRPC investigation include the following:

Section 154: First Information Report (FIR)[67] - This section explains how the police officer in charge of the police station should proceed when learning that a cognizable offence has been committed.

Section 156: Investigation of Cognizable Offences[68] - This section gives police officers the authority to conduct investigations into cognizable offences without a magistrate's approval.

Section 157: Procedure for Investigation - This section specifies the steps that must be taken to conduct an investigation, including questioning witnesses and seizing property.

Section 161: Witness Examination - This section permits the police to question witnesses during a case investigation.

Section 162: Police Statements No Statement to be Signed - This clause forbids the police from receiving a statement that has been signed from anyone during the course of the investigation.

Section 172: Diary of Proceedings in Investigation - This provision mandates that the police officer overseeing the investigation keep a diary of the events as they occur.

Section 173: Report of Investigation - This provision mandates that, after the investigation is complete, the police officer present a report of the investigation to the magistrate.

Section 174: Suicide Investigation, etc. - The police officer is given the authority to look into incidents of unnatural death or suicide under this clause.

Section 175: Power to Summon Persons[69] - Under this section, a police officer has the authority to call any individual to testify during an investigation.

Section 176: Inquiry by Magistrate into Cause of Death - In circumstances of unnatural death or suicide, this section allows the magistrate to inquire into the cause of death.

Section 207: Supply of Documents to Accused[70] - According to this section, the magistrate must provide copies of all documents, including the investigation report, to the accused upon request.

Commitment of Case to Sessions Court - Section 208 This section covers the case's commitment to the sessions court following the conclusion of the investigation.

These legislative guidelines provide the parameters for criminal offence investigations in India and guarantee a just and unbiased inquiry process.

4: Abuses of Power by Police During Investigation

Police misconduct during an investigation can take many different forms, including:

- *Illegal detention*: Police personnel may keep suspects in custody for longer than is allowed by law or without a valid reason.

- *Physical Abuse:* Beatings, torture, or other physical violence inflicted on the suspect are all examples of physical abuse.

- *Forced confessions*: Even if a suspect is innocent, police may employ force, threats, or psychological pressure to get a confession from them.

  Fabrication of Evidence: Police officers may create evidence or tamper with already-existing evidence to accuse the innocent.

- *Privacy invasion*: Police may search and seize property without a warrant or other valid legal justification, as well as violate a suspect's privacy in other ways.

- *Violation of Privacy:* Police may abuse surveillance technologies and other means to invade people's privacy or violate their civil rights.

---

[70] GIRIRAJ SHAH, THE INDIAN POLICE- A RETROSPECT, 9, (Himalaya Publishing House, Bombay, 1992).

- *Discrimination*: Rather than looking for evidence of wrongdoing, police may target people based on their race, ethnicity, religion, or other traits.

In addition to violating people's rights, these power abuses also compromise the fairness of the criminal justice system. Holding police officials responsible for any abuses of authority committed during investigations is crucial, as is ensuring that the necessary processes are followed to preserve suspects' rights.

DETERMINATIVE PARAMETERS TO DECIDE THE DEFECTIVE OR IMPROPER INVESTIGATION:

When addressing the question of a poor or unethical inquiry conducted by the responsible investigating officials, who are required by statute to undertake those tasks, court in *Dayal Singh & Ors,* v. *State of Uttaranchal*[71] formulated some deciding variables in the following manner,[72]"

(i)   if there were omissions or commissions that culminated in an illegal or deficient inquiry;

(ii)   If those standard and/or actions of omissions and commissions harmed the government's matter

(iii)   If the default and actions in question is voluntary, accidental, or the product of inevitable conditions in a particular instance

(iv)   If the abuse of power and failure to comply is intentional, is the court required to provide reasonable orders, namely instructions authorizing the initiation of criminal or other civil proceedings against the officer/witness

The Supreme Court noted that the investigative officer is required to be "diligent, honest, and impartial in their methodology and inquiry.".[73] Concerning the consequences of the 'actions or omissions that culminated in abuse' on the lawsuit, the court stated that considering the effects is completely meaningless. It is not required that any abuse result in bias to the prosecution's argument. Only the investigative cop's intentional conduct or

---

[71]   2012 SCC OnLine SC 580
[72]   *Justice M.L Singhal, Volume 2, Sohoni's Code of Criminal Procedure,1973, 22nd edition.*
[73]   Dayal Singh & Ors, v. State of Uttaranchal, 2012 SCC OnLine SC 580 at para 21

reckless behaviour is necessary to establish that the lead investigator abused his or her investigative authority.

In *State of Punjab* v. *Ram Singh*[74]"The effects of these lapses could usually be due to negligence," he noted. However, an intended exclusion or commission succeeds in a purposefully flawed inquiry. The court stated that in the event of wilful[75] dereliction of duty, performing an inquiry in an insensitive and reckless way, the court has the authority to make clear findings justifying the initiation of an examination against the involved law enforcement officer and directing for disciplinary action.

Unsympathetic Disinclination to Register A Case: **In** *Mohindro v.   of Punjab*[76], the State contended that because the claim lacked legitimacy, police began an investigation without reporting the event. While guiding for certification of the complaint, the Supreme Court benches stated that the supposed evidence strongly show that, despite the appellant's application to the police for identification, the police refused to record the specific instance for no cause.

In *Lallan Choudhary and ors* v. *State of Bihar and Anr*[77],

While a case under Section 452/323/34 was reported, one under Section 395 was not, despite the fact that the report included charges for the same. The Supreme Court has held that failing to record a FIR in the event of a punishable offense resulted in a wrongful conviction, and that the relevant police officer performed a serious gross injustice by refusing to record the FIR for which he is lawfully required.

The court noted, "The FIR filed by the Police made it abundantly evident that the petition for a charged under Section 395 IPC was intentionally withheld, and thus, no inquiry for the charged under Section 395 IPC was undertaken.

---

[74] (1992) 4 SCC 54.
[75] ibid
[76] 3 (2001) 9 SCC 581].
[77] Lallan Choudhary v. State of Bihar(2006) 12 SCC 229 at para 11.

Brutality of Police

- 25 March 1966 – Pravir Chandra Bhanj Deo, Pravir, King of Bastar, was the state's twentieth Maharaja and was assassinated in 1966 for promoting his subjects' demand. He struggled for the indigenous individuals's interests regarding the 1957 national election; he served the Jagdalpur Vidhan Sabha division in the unwavering Madhya Pradesh National Legislature.[78]

- 1979 to 1980 – The Bhagalpur blinding occurred in Bhagalpur, Bihar, India, in which police disabled 31 suspects (or accused criminals, according to a few accounts) by forcing acids into their eyes.

- 11 January 1982 – The Bombay Cop's first contact has concluded. Manya Surve, a mob boss from Kiriti College in Bombay[79], was assassinated. Five shots were shot into his chest and shoulder, and he died instantly. Shootout at Wadala is a film focused on this true story.

- 22 May 1987 – The Hashimpura tragedy happened during the Hindu-Muslim clashes in Meerut, Uttar Pradesh[80], India, when 19 members of the Regional Paramilitary Constabulary allegedly summarily executed Muslim youngsters from the city's Hashimpura mohalla (particular state), transported them in a vehicle to the suburbs, near Murad Nagar in the Ghaziabad district, where they were shot and their corpses deposited in a water cistern. A few days back, corpses were discovered submerged in canals.

- 1–2 October 1994 – On the night of 1–2 October 1994, police opened fire on helpless Uttarakhand revolutionaries at Rampur Tiraha (crossing) in the Muzaffarnagar[81] area of Uttar Pradesh India. The revolutionaries were on their way to Delhi to stage a dharna at Raj Ghat on Gandhi Jayanti the next morning when suspected unjustified officers fired in the evening of 1 October resulted in the loss of six campaigners, and many females were reportedly harassed and sexually abused during the subsequent melee.

- 2003 – The Muthanga incident involved a violent law enforcement operation against Adivasis who had assembled under the banner of Adivasi Gothra

---

[78] 1961 AIR 775

[79] 6 Kuldova, Tereza. "designing hypermuscular neo-aristocracy: of kings, gangsters and muscles in Indian cinema, fashion and politics." Film, Fashion & Consumption 3.2 (2014): 149-156.

[80] Graff, Violette, and Juliette Galonnier. "Hindu-Muslim Communal Riots in India II (1986-2011)." Online Encyclopedia of Mass Violence, Paris, Sciences Po, CERI (2012).

[81] Rawat, R. UTTARAKHAND'S AWAKENING: COLLECTED ARTICLES.

Mahasabha (ADMS) in disapproval against the Kerala Government's[82] pause in allocating land negotiated in October 2001. Formally, two deaths were verified; however, the authorities subsequently revised the casualty count to five. About 15 Adivasis have been mortally injured.

- 2007 – Policemen decided to open gunfire on protesters against the Salim Group's purchase of property for a chemistry center in Nandigram villages in East Midnapore, West Bengal.[83] • 2009 – During a religious confrontation in the fishing village Beemapally in Trivandrum District, Kerala, policemen unleashed firing on Muslims, killing six and wounding

- 23 July 2009 – At Imphal's Khwairamband area, Manipur cop soldiers murdered an innocent teenager Ch Sanjit Meitei in a suspected confrontation and later reported to have seized a gun from him; in the subsequent confrontation a pregnant woman Rabina Devi was also assassinated, the police saying she was fired in the firefight.

- June 3, 2011 – Four villagers were shot to death Forbesganj, a city in Bihar, India, in an incident of government violence known as the Forbesganj shooting[84]. ANHAD, a renowned NGO, launched an investigation into the event and concluded that leaders from the Bhartiya Janata Party were involved in the massacres. Occupants of Bhajanpur community were opposing the number of resources to a plant operated by the son of BJP leader Ashok Agarwal.

- 25 August 2015 – The Patidar group rallied over 500,000 citizens at Ahmedabad's 43GMDC Grounds, requesting OBC quo*ta*. Hardik Patel, the chairperson, led those who remained on starvation diet after the conclusion of the structured protest. Police detained him in the night, using a lathicharge that wounded many reporters.

- 2015 – The Andhra shooting was an event in the Seshachalam forest in the Andhra Pradesh district of Chittoor that resulted in the death of twenty alleged lumberjacks.

- 2018 – Thoothukudi Rampage (also identified as Thoothukudi shooting, Thoothukudi officers fired, Sterlite protester shooting, and others) refers to incidents that occurred on 22 and 23 May 2018 in Thoothukudi, Tamil Nadu,

[82] 0 Haseena, V. A. "Land alienation and livelihood problems of scheduled tribes in Kerala." Research on Humanities and Social Science 4.10 (2014): 76-81.
[83] 1 McConnochie, Adam. "'The Blessed Land': Narratives of Peasant Resistance at Nandigram, West Bengal, in 2007." (2012).
[84] Bhattacharya, Dipankar. "Ranvir Sena Revisited: Feudal-Kulak Power and Lalu-Nitish Continuum." Economic and Political Weekly (2012): 15-19.

India. The shooting started as part of a massive protest against Sterlite Company's planned extension of a copper smelter project in Thoothukudi city. Policemen opened firing on demonstrators, killing 13 and injuring 102. Additionally, many security officers were killed during the demonstrations.

- 2019 – After the Citizenship Amendment Act demonstrations in 201947, police targeted both activist demonstrators and non-protesting students on the Jamia Milia Islamia site. In the same week, policemen and Rapid Action Force officers wounded many students — along with many who sustained severe injury — by shooting tear-gas bombs, rubber shots stun grenades, and projectiles at protesters at Aligarh Muslim University who were opposing the same act. According to reports, armed personnel shouted racial epithets at the participants. The powers shot tear gas shells into hostel bedrooms and caught alight to student cars.

On 19 June, both were arrested after a FIR was lodged against them. Even so, the CBI argued in its case filed that no breach of Lockdown occurred. They were physically molested and humiliated by police after their detention, which resulted in their fatalities. Bennicks became sick on 22 June 2020 and was sent to Kovilpatti Medical Center, where he succumbed to death later that day. His dad expired the next day, 22 June 2020. The two male's custodial deaths in Tamil Nadu's Sathankulam town in the Thoothukudi district have ignited widespread uproar in the state about policing violence In Sheela Barsev. Union of India, [85] The Apex Court stated that since a kid is a national possession it is the government's responsibility to watch after it in order to ensure the child's maximum growth of personalities. That is why all laws governing children guarantee that no infant shall be imprisoned. Without a question, imprisonment will stunt the child's growth, expose him to harmful stimuli, coarsen his morality, and alienate him from community.

The Supreme Court issued the following directives[86]:

1. Before initiating an inquiry, it is critical that the evidence included in the FIR reveal all of the components that define a punishable offense.

2. Investigative authorities must be conducted strictly in compliance with legal protections and statutory requirements.

---

[85] AIR 1986 SC 1773
[86] 0State of West Bengal v.Swapan Kumar Guha & Others(1982) SCC 561

3. Courts have an obligation to participate in the inquiry mechanism to protect victims against abuse if their privileges are abused and proper practice is not practiced. Law enforcement officers also feel resistance to file charges based on shoddy evidence.

The Apex Court has established that a proper compromise must be found between civilians' constitutional rights and the cop's broad authority to prosecute an offense.[87]

In the matter of T.T. *Anthony* v. *State of Kerala*

Concerning the prosecution of offenses, the essential details of which are as follows:

53 Five people were murdered and many others wounded in a well-known incident in Kerala's Kannur district. The attack was launched to disperse opposing demonstrators opposing the presence of a representative from the governing UDF alliance. Eight listed and several unnamed members of the opposing group were charged with causing the protests that prompted the police violence. In the meantime, in response to widespread outrage, the UDF Government launched an investigation into the event.

The UDF lost the referendum in the interim, and the opposition took over. The Commission of Inquiry's investigation, which was published after the new government's election victory, blamed the Executive Commissioner and the Deputy Commissioner of Security for the killings..

5: Relevant Cases with Regard to Investigation

The inquiry process and technique have been significantly impacted by a number of big cases that have occurred in India. Some of the more pertinent examples include:

In the case of *D.K. Basu* v. *State of West Bengal*,[88] rules were created for arresting and holding people, including the need to explain the circumstances of the arrest and give the accused person access to legal representation.

In the case of *Maneka Gandhi* v. *Union of India*[89], the right to personal liberty under Article 21 of the Indian Constitution was established, and the significance of due process in criminal trials was emphasised.

---

[87]   T.T. Anthony v. State of Kerala, AIR 2001 SC 2637.
[88]   AIR 1997 SC 610.
[89]   AIR 1978 SC 597

Gujarat State v. *Zahira Habibullah Sheikh*[90]: This case demonstrated the importance of witness protection and the risks associated with witness intimidation in high-profile cases.

In the case of *Kharak Singh v. State of Uttar Pradesh*[91], the right to privacy was acknowledged as a fundamental freedom and restrictions on police surveillance were created.

In the case of *R.K. Dalmia v. Delhi Administration*, it was decided that evidence collected unlawfully could not be utilised in court proceedings.

These cases have had a significant impact on the criminal justice system in India and have served to set key ideas and rules for the investigation process there.

---

[90]   2004 (5) SCC 353
[91]   AIR (1963) SC 1295.

CHAPTER 5
RECOMMENDATION OF VARIOUS COMMITTEES
ON POLICE REFORM

1: Gore Committee on Police Training 1971 – 1973

Initiated in 1971, the Gore Committee on Police Training delivered its final report in 1973. The committee's principal objective was to evaluate the current police officer training programmes and suggest improvements.

The following are some of the committee's main recommendations:

- Creation of a centralised police officer training facility.

- Incorporating new criminology, forensic science, and scientific investigation courses into the training programmes.

- Putting a focus on the value of human rights and the necessity of preserving public confidence in the police.

- Enhancing police officers' physical preparedness and martial arts instruction.

- Increasing the length of training courses for both new recruits and officers already in the field.

- Promoting the use of cutting-edge tools and technologies in police training.

- Expanding the opportunity for hands-on instruction and practical practise.

The Gore Committee made recommendations to enhance police training and give police personnel the knowledge and abilities they need to perform their tasks successfully.

Later, the suggestions served as the foundation for the creation of fresh training curricula for Indian police officers.

2: National Police Commission (NPC) 1977–1981[92]

The Indian government established the National Police Commission (NPC) in 1977 to review the nation's police force and suggest any required changes. Between 1979 and 1981, the NPC delivered eight reports that included a thorough set of suggestions for police changes. Among the NPC's main suggestions are:

- The creation of an independent complaints authority to look into and address complaints against the police.

- To achieve more effectiveness and accountability, the police should separate its law enforcement and investigation departments.

- Construction of a central police university for instruction and study.

- The establishment of an all-India Police Cadre for the purpose of hiring and elevating police officers[93].

- Putting in place a tenure system for senior police personnel to stop transfers as often and guarantee.

- To assist with investigation and crime prevention, a national database of criminals and their actions should be created.

- Ensure that women and members of underrepresented groups are fairly represented in the police force.

- policing operations are being made more efficient, and technology and equipment are being updated.

Although the NPC's recommendations were thorough, many of them have not yet been fully implemented, and the Indian police system still faces numerous difficulties.

---

92   *S.N. Mishra, The code of criminal procedure, 1973, 21st edition.*
93   Law Commission of India, 154th Report on the Code of Criminal Procedure, 1973 (22 August, 1996).

3: Ribeiro Committee on Police Reforms (1998-1999)

To make recommendations for changes to the Indian police system, the Ribeiro Committee on Police Reforms was established in 1998. Julio Ribeiro, a retired Indian Police Service officer, served as the committee's chairman[94]. A number of recommendations were included in the report the committee submitted in 1999 with the goal of strengthening the police department's accountability and operational efficiency.

The following were some of the main suggestions put forth by the Ribeiro Committee:

- Investigation and law and order tasks should be separated, according to the committee's recommendation, in order to improve accountability and efficiency within the police force.

- Police force modernization: The committee suggested that the police force be updated with the newest tools and technology to improve its effectiveness.

- Proper training for police officers: In order to increase their professionalism, the committee suggested that police officers receive proper training in community policing, human rights, and investigations[95].

- The committee proposed that community policing be promoted in order to improve relations between the police and the community.

- In order to promote more responsibility within the police force, the committee advised the creation of an independent system to look into complaints against police officers.

In India Emergencies to establish the Shah Commission of Inquiry,there has been much discussion and disagreement about the Ribeiro Committee on Police Reforms' recommendations. Many of the recommendations have yet to be implemented, however some have already been.

---

[94] Police Reforms in India; An analytical study by K. Alexander, 2006, p1
[95] 2 Op.cit. Police Reforms in India, p 7

4: Padmanabhaiah Committee on Police Reforms (2000)

The Padmanabhaiah Committee on Police Reforms was established in 2000 to examine how the Indian police operate and make recommendations for modernising and reforming them.

In its 2000 report, the committee offered a number of suggestions, including[96]:

- In order to prevent the state government from having an undue influence on the police, state security commissions (SSCs) should be established.

- Separation between the police's investigative and law enforcement missions.

- Strengthening the Central Bureau of Investigation's (CBI) capacity to look into important national cases.

- Establishing a separate complaints authority to look into allegations of police misconduct.

- the creation of a Police Establishment Board (PEB) to control police officer promotions, postings, and transfers.

- Civil society participation and the introduction of community policing.

- Enhancing police officers' working circumstances, including their housing, education, and tools.

- The committee's suggestions were made with the intention of increasing the efficacy, accountability, and efficiency of the Indian police force. Police reform in India is still a hotly debated topic despite the fact that many of the suggestions have not been put into action.

5: Malimath Committee on Reforms of Criminal Justice System (2001–2003)

The Malimath Committee was established by the Indian government in 2000 to review and recommend changes to the country's criminal justice system. *Justice V.S. Malimath,* a retired judge from India's Supreme Court, served as the committee's chairman.

---

[96] PIB press release dated 22.07.2015 on Model Police Act.

In 2003, the committee delivered its report, which included more than 150 recommendations for changes in policing, inquiries, prosecutions, and trials, among other areas of the criminal justice system.

- The following were some of the Malimath Committee's main recommendations:

- The creation of a National Judicial Service to handle judicial officer hiring, training, and appointment.

- The adoption of plea bargaining as a substitute strategy for adjudicating disputes in criminal cases.

- Establishing a distinct investigation team to look into major crimes like terrorism, organised crime, and economic offenses.

- To enhance the standard of the inquiry, a network of forensic science laboratories should be established.

- The use of contemporary technology for trials and other judicial proceedings, such as video conferencing, email, and fax.

- The establishment of witness protection programmes to guarantee their security during criminal investigations.

- Implementing a victim-focused strategy in the criminal justice system.

However, the government has not acted on several of the Malimath Committee's recommendations, which has led to ongoing criticism of how India's criminal justice system operates.

6: Police Act Drafting Committee (2005–2006)

The Ministry of Home Affairs, Government of India, established the Police legislation Drafting Committee (PADC) in 2005 with the task of creating a new model police legislation. The committee, which was led by *Justice (Retd.) V.S. Malimath*, included people from the criminal justice system, academia, and civil society. In its 2006 report, the committee made several recommendations for changes to increase the effectiveness and accountability of the police[97].

The PADC made several important recommendations, including the creation of a State Security Commission to oversee police operations, a Police Establishment Board to ensure transparency in police transfers and promotions, and a separate investigation division within the police force. The committee also suggested that police officers receive better training and working conditions, as well as the implementation of contemporary technologies for crime prevention and investigation.

However, not all Indian states have embraced the model police statute that the PADC advocated, and some of the suggested reforms have not been put into place. Despite this, the PADC report continues to make a significant contribution to the conversation in India about police reforms[98].

---

[97] India. Rajya Sabha Unstarred Question No. 1975 dated 18.12.2015.
[98] Op.cit. Status note on police reforms, p4

CHAPTER 6
JUDICIAL CONTRIBUTION TO THE POLICE
SYSTEM IN INDIA: AND A CASE STUDY
OF THE PRAKASH SINGH

Case 1: Introduction to Judicial Contribution to Police System

The functioning of the police system in India has been significantly shaped by the country's courts. Every citizen in India is given fundamental rights under the Indian Constitution, and the court guards these rights. The courts have issued a number of significant rulings over the years that have had a significant impact on India's police system. These rulings seek to promote police accountability, lessen police power abuse, and enhance the police force's efficiency in upholding law and order.

The Prakash Singh case[99], which resulted in significant changes to the police system and set the ground for police reforms in India, was one such landmark decision. The Supreme Court ordered the federal and state governments to put into effect a number of police reform guidelines in this case.

The ruling was a substantial advancement in the direction of improved police effectiveness, accountability, and community relations. In-depth analysis of the Prakash Singh case and discussion of its effects on India's police system will be provided in this case study.

Context: A father-son pair, P. Jeyaraj (58) and Fenix (31) respectively, perished in police detention in Tamil Nadu, bringing the sad plight of the Indian police system to the fore once more. Families and protesters worry that there has been police brutality in this case. They were detained because they operated their store past the curfew (which was imposed in light of COVID-19 regulations)[100].

---

[99] Prakash Singh & Ors vs Union Of India And Ors on 22 September, 2006
[100] S.N. Misra, The Code of Criminal Procedure 1973 10 (Central Law Publications, Allahabad, 15th edn., 2008).

The Police System is a vestige of colonialism. Immediately following the mutiny in 1857, the first Police commission was established. In 1861, the First Indian Police Act was passed.

The first national commission established following independence was the *National Police Committee in 1978*[101].

Its terms of reference were broad and included the police organisation, as well as its purpose, accountability, and relationships with the general public.

Between 1979 and 1981, it produced eight reports, including the Model Police Act. But the majority of the NCP's recommendations have not been carried out.

Risk to life: There is a significant risk to life in the police. More police officers are killed in the line of duty in India than any other nation in the world. There is no indication that the risk component would decrease in the future.

Police Infrastructure: The firearms, vehicles, and other equipment used by the police force at a lower level are outmoded and inadequate in comparison to the contemporary firearms utilised by criminals and antisocial elements[102].

Police staff qualifications and training: The methods used to teach police are obsolete, and training modules primarily disregard human rights issues.

Police officers receive instruction that is skewed substantially in their advantage. The training of IPS officers accounts for 94% of all training expenses.

Inhumane investigative methods like the third degree, which involves hammering iron nails into the body, beating the soles of the feet, stretching the legs apart in opposite directions, hitting the private area, and other draconian acts, are the result of unscientific criminal investigation techniques and a lack of training in human rights.

massive vacancies The Indian police have been overworked and outnumbered more than in many western democracies due to the spectacular growth of the territory that has to be policed and the rise in the number of lives that need to be protected. In comparison to most

---

[101] State of Karnataka v. Selvi J. Jayalalitha & Ors, (2017) 6 SCC 263.
[102] Zahira Habibullah H. Sheikh v. State of Gujarat, 2005 Cr LJ 2050 (S.C.).

contemporary democracies, there are just 140 policeman for every 100,000 citizens, an extremely low ratio.

Police are overworked, especially at lower levels when they are required to work nonstop for 14–16 hours a day.

Because of political cases brought by the ruling parties against their rivals and because of undue political intervention by the political executives, CID has struggled to function at the state level[103].

The police force is unable to maintain law and order as a result of a lack of coordination between the federal government and the states. Due to ego conflicts and unfathomable personal differences, the dual command at the district and state levels has made it difficult to coordinate between civil servants and police personnel.

Ineffectiveness against new types of crime: Due to structural flaws, the police force is not equipped to deal with modern issues like cybercrime, international terrorism, and naxalism.

Underutilization of modernization funds: States and centres both allot money for state police force modernization. These money are often used to build new police stations, buy weapons, communication tools, and vehicles, enhancing the infrastructure of the police. However, the underutilization of modernization money has remained a concern[104].

Current Corruption Because of their extremely poor pay, especially at the lower ranks, police officers are compelled to use corrupt methods to support themselves. Because the Rank system is prevalent among the police force, upper-level executives misuse their power over lower-level employees.

---

[103] Bikram Jeet Batra, "Public Prosecution in Need of Reform", India Together, July 5, 2005, available at: (last visited on June 10, 2019)
[104] Om Prakash V. State Of Uttar Pradesh, 2009 Cri.L.J. 782

2: Role of the Judiciary in Police Reform in India

India's judiciary has made a substantial contribution to police reform. Numerous landmark decisions by the Supreme Court and High Courts have emphasised the necessity of police reform and have given the federal and state governments orders to put those reforms into effect[105].

The Prakash Singh case from 2006 represents the most significant court contribution to police reform in India. Former police officers Prakash Singh and N.K. Singh brought the lawsuit in an effort to address the lack of police accountability and the inability to carry through past recommendations for police reform.

The Supreme Court ordered the federal and state governments to carry out a number of measures, including the creation of a State Security Commission, a Police Complaints Authority, and the division of the police's investigation and law and order functions, in its ruling, to ensure police accountability and effectiveness.

In addition to the Prakash Singh case, other significant rulings that have influenced police reform in India include the *DK Basu case (1997)*, which established standards for arrest and detention of people, and the NHRC case (1997), which emphasised the need for police reform and instructed the federal and state governments to take a number of steps to ensure police accountability and effectiveness.

In India, the judiciary has played a significant role in promoting police reform and guaranteeing that the police operate in a fair, just, and responsible manner.

3: Analysis of the Prakash Singh Case

A significant incident in India's history of police reforms is the Prakash Singh case. Former IPS officer Prakash Singh and others filed a Public Interest Litigation (PIL) in 1996 against the Union of India and others, requesting guidelines for the implementation of the seven orders issued by the Supreme Court in the D.K. Basu case regarding arrest and detention of individuals.

---

[105] Vakil Prasad Singh V. State Of Bihar, 2009 Cri.L.J. 1731

A three-judge Supreme Court panel heard the case and rendered a landmark decision on September 22, 2006. The ruling mandated the implementation of the seven instructions issued in the D.K. Basu case, in addition to other police reform recommendations made by various bodies[106].

The Supreme Court issued seven orders in the D.K. Basu case, and they are as follows:

- The police should explain the reasons for the arrest to the individual being held as well as the person's right to have someone else informed of the arrest.

- Within 24 hours of their arrest, the person should appear before a magistrate.

- A medical officer should check on the person who has been arrested at the moment of the arrest and then every 48 hours after that.

- During questioning, the detained person should be given permission to speak with his or her attorney.

- A memo should be written down that includes the place, time, and identity of the arresting officer.

- At least one witness, who could be a relative or a local person, must attest to the arrest memo.

- A person arrested or detained should be allowed to meet his/her family members and friends.

A State Security Commission was mandated to be established by the Prakash Singh case ruling in order to establish guidelines and set rules for the effective and efficient operation of the police force.

Additionally, it ordered the establishment of a National Security Commission by the federal government to compile a list of candidates for the selection and appointment of the leaders of the central police organisations.

The Prakash Singh case had a key role in fundamentally altering how India's police department operated.

---

[106] Prakash Singh v. Union of India, Writ Petition (Civil) No. 310 of 1996, (2006) 8 SCC 1.

4: Assessment of Police Reforms in India after the Prakash Singh Case

Numerous initiatives to improve the Indian police force have been launched since the historic Prakash Singh case in 2006[107]. Among the important initiatives and reforms implemented are:

- **Setting up State Security**: The Supreme Court ordered all the states to create State Security Commissions (SSCs) in order to ensure that the state government did not exert improper pressure or influence on the police. SSCs are in charge of creating the policies and procedures necessary for the police to operate effectively.

- **Police Complaints Authorities (PCAs):** The court had instructed the states to create PCAs at the state and district levels. PCAs receive and look into allegations of police misconduct, then suggest the best course of action.

- **Separation of Investigation and Law and Order Functions**: Investigation and law and order functions should be clearly separated in the police force, according to a court decision, in order to prevent conflicts of interest and guarantee fair and unbiased investigations.

- **Police Training:** The court has advocated raising the standard of police training, including initial, ongoing, and specialised training.

- **Community policing:** To improve police-public relations and promote trust between the police and the community, the court had suggested that community policing be implemented.

- **Use of technologies**: To increase the effectiveness and efficiency of the police force, the court had advised using modern tools like GPS, CCTVs, and other technologies.

In spite of the Supreme Court's orders and instructions in the Prakash Singh case, India's police reforms have been implemented slowly and unevenly. While some states have made an effort to put the suggested reforms into place, others have not. To implement large and thorough police reforms in India, ongoing efforts and political commitment are required.

---

[107] 6Compliance with Supreme Court Directives on Police Reforms, Commonwealth Human Rights Initiative (CHRI), 30th November 2016,

5: Supreme Court's directives for avoidance of Custodial crime

In order to prevent crimes committed while in custody and to guarantee the protection of human rights, the Indian Supreme Court has issued a number of orders. Among the crucial instructions are:

- The guidelines outlined in Sections 41, 41A, 41B, 41C, and 41D of the Criminal Procedure Code, 1973 must be followed when making any arrests.

- Within 24 hours of being detained, the suspect must be brought before a magistrate and notified of the reason(s) for his arrest[108].

- The person who has been arrested has the right to retain legal counsel and defence.

- The person who has been arrested has a right to be informed of his arrest.

- The arrestee or a witness must sign the memo of arrest that the police must compile at the time of the arrest.

- Every 48 hours while in custody, the arrestee must have a medical check-up by a licenced physician.

- The person who has been arrested must countersign a police registry of those who have been detained.

- All deaths in custody must be reported by the police to the National Human Rights Commission within 24 hours.

- The entire arrest and questioning process must be captured on camera by the police, and the magistrate and the accused's attorney must have access to this tape.

- The accused cannot be subjected to any type of torture or other cruel, barbaric, or degrading treatment, according to the police.

- Any police officer who disobeys these orders shall be immediately punished.

---

[108] The National Police Commission: Some Selected Recommendations of the National Police Commission, CHRI, http://humanrightsinitiative.org/old/publications/police/npc_recommendations.pdf. (last visited Aug 23, 2018).

These guidelines are meant to safeguard human rights and deter crimes committed while in custody. The Supreme Court has emphasised that the police must completely abide by these instructions, and that any violations will be dealt with harshly.

6: Judicial Response on violation of human rights by Police

When it comes to examples of police misconduct that violated human rights, the Indian judiciary has been vigilant. When it has been determined that the police have infringed someone's human rights, the judiciary has taken stern action against the culprits. The judicial system has also taken proactive steps to avoid these infractions in the first place.

The Supreme Court of India set thorough instructions for police arrests and detentions of people in *D.K. Basu v. State of West Bengal* (1997). The rules were created to protect the rights of people who had been arrested and to prohibit violence towards inmates. In addition to instructing the arrestee of their right to legal representation, the court ordered that a memo of arrest be created at the time of the arrest. The arrestee must appear before a magistrate within 24 hours and undergo a medical check-up after being detained, according to the court's orders.

The judiciary has recently been heavily involved in overseeing police encounter cases, which have frequently come under fire for being extrajudicial in nature. The Supreme Court has established a number of panels to look into these matters and has instructed the police to adhere to due process when necessary.

CHAPTER 7
LEGAL PROVISIONS RELATING TO POLICE

1: The Police Act, 1861

In India, the organisation, authority, and management of police forces are governed by the Police Act of 1861. The act was passed during the British colonial era and is still in effect, albeit having undergone numerous amendments.

The following are some of the main clauses of the Police Act of 1861:

- *Creating a police force:* The statute mandates the creation of a police force in every state.

- *Police Responsibility:* Police responsibilities are outlined in the act and include maintaining law and order, protecting people's lives and property, and preserving the peace in addition to preventing and identifying crimes.

- *Police officer appointments*: The act outlines the procedures for appointing police officials, including the director general of police and other senior officers.

- *Police officers' authority* outlined in the act, and this authority includes the right to conduct property searches, make arrests, and investigate and prevent crime.

- *Police supervision and control:* The statute stipulates that both the state and federal governments may supervise and regulate the police.

- *Police accountability*: The legislation outlines the police's responsibilities to the public and the government, including the creation of complaint bodies to look into allegations against police officers.

- *Police regulations*: The act calls for the creation of police regulations to control how the police are run and how officers behave.

The Police Act of 1861 has drawn criticism for its colonial-era provisions, lack of accountability and transparency, and insufficient protections for human rights. To address these problems, requests for police reform and the adoption of new laws have grown in recent years[109].

In September 2005, the Ministry of Home Affairs of the Government of India established a Committee of Experts under the chairmanship of Dr. Soli J. Sorabjee, a former Attorney General of the Government of India, to draught a new Police Act that could address, among other things, the escalating challenges to policing and to satisfy the democratic aspirations of the populace. In light of the difficulties and the shifting role and responsibilities of the police, the Committee was given the duty of drafting a new Police Act.

The extent and definitions are covered in Chapter I. This chapter's definitions of terminology are thorough and provide a comprehensive grasp of the sections that come before section 2.

The organisation of the police force is covered in Chapter II.

It covers the choice of police officers and their terms of office. It states that the State Government shall choose the Director General of Police or Inspector General, and that his tenure of office shall be for four years[110].

The State Government, acting in consultation with the State Security Commission (which has been covered in Chapter III)[111], may, however, relieve the DGP/IG of his duties if there is any action taken against him under the All India Services (Discipline and Appeal) Rules, he is found guilty in court of a criminal offence or a case of corruption, or if he is otherwise incapable of performing his duties. By noting the upkeep of forensic laboratories and the organising of research, this chapter considers recent scientific developments and how they are helpful to the police.

The Act acknowledges that the state government must have oversight of the police after taking these directives into account.

---

109 National Police Commission, NPC: Sixth Report Para 48.15 (2018).
110Summary of Ribeiro Committee's Recommendations, CHRI, https:// humanrightsinitiative .org/old/publications/police/recommendations_ribeiro.pdf. (last visited on 22nd Aug 2018).
111 Summary of Recommendations made by the Padmanabhaiah Committee on Police Reforms, CHRI, http://humanrightsinitiative.org/programs/aj/police/india/initiatives/summary_padmanabhaiah.pdf. (last visited on 22nd Aug 2018). 8The Padhmanabhaiah Committee On Police Reforms, Lexpress, https://lexpress.in/criminal-justice/the-padmanabhaiah-committeeon-police-reforms. (last visited on 22nd July 2018).

But in *chapter III*, it recommended the formation of a statutory agency called the State Security Commission to combat the existence of undue dominant influence. The State Security Commission would be headed by the Minister in charge of the police, and its other members would be the Chief Minister, two members of the State Legislature—one from the ruling party and the other from the opposition—and four retired judges of distinction who would be nominated by the Chief Minister and approved by the State Legislature. The State Security Commission is in charge of establishing broad policy guidelines and directives for the execution of various police functions as well as for the evaluation and ongoing monitoring of police operations.

The Commission is also responsible for hearing complaints from police personnel who hold ranks equal to or higher than Superintendent of Police regarding receiving improper or illegal orders while doing their responsibilities. In contrast to police legislation in the UK, South Africa, Canada, and Northern Ireland, the Police Act of 1861 does not provide any mechanisms to ensure external accountability[112]. The new police Act restricts itself to defining appraisal of police performance and generally maintaining track of police operations as duties of the State Security Commission.

The Act's section 38 mandates that a Director of Inspection assess police performance and report findings to the State Security Commission. In the UK, a Police Standards Unit evaluates and compares the performance of various forces based on the Police Performance Assessment Framework (PPAF), which is produced annually by the Home Office. The PPAF evaluates police performance based on a number of variables, including: public perception of local police performing well in the British Crime Survey; satisfaction of victims of racist incidents with the service provided by the police; satisfaction of victims of domestic burglary, violent crime, vehicle crime, and road traffic collisions with respect to police handling of their cases; Incidence (per 1000 people) of home burglaries, violent crime, robberies, vehicle crime, life-threatening and firearms crime; Representation of Women and Minorities in the Force; Number and percentage of crimes prosecuted; response to domestic abuse cases; data on fatalities or serious injuries from traffic accidents; public impression of crime fear; time lost because of police officers' illness, etc[113].

---

[112] Shankar Gopalakrishnan, Recommendations Of The Malimath Committee On Reforms Of Criminal Justice System,PEOPLE'S UNION FOR CIVIL LIBERTIES, Pucl.Org, 2018, http://www.pucl.org/Topics/Law/2003/malimath-recommendations.htm. (Last visited on 22 July 2018)

[113] Sony Kunjappan, A Review on "The Model Police Bill 2015"- Proposed to the Parliament of India,

The Act's *Chapter IV* discusses the roles, responsibilities, and authority of the police. The overall transition from Power and Authority to Role and Functions, Duties, Social Responsibilities, and Emergency Duties in this Chapter is a good one.

The new Act's *Chapter V* is the only section that specifically addresses disciplinary actions. The old Police Act of 1861 gives the Inspector General, Deputy Inspectors General, Assistant Inspectors General, and District Superintendents of Police the authority to fire, suspend, or demote any police officer of the lower ranks they believe to be unfit for the position or has been remiss or negligent in the performance of their duties. The number of disciplinary sanctions that can be applied to police officers has increased under the new Act of 2007. Outright dismissal, removal from service, rank decrease, loss of approved service, pay reduction, etc. are a few of them[114].

The police regulations are discussed in *Chapter VI*. In this chapter, some distinctly novel aspects of the police job can be found. In comparison to what the 1861 Police Act envisioned, the police now have a larger and more proactive preventive role.

The UK's Police Reforms Act[115], 2002 permits people to use their police authority. It grants the chiefs of police the ability to select civilians to serve as community support officers and gives them the authority to deal with anti-social activity.

Special measures for maintaining public order and state security are covered in Chapter VII. In essence, it deals with the deployment of additional police officers as needed.

Despite being the Act's smallest chapter, *Chapter VIII* is one of the most crucial ones. It states that the district magistrate and executive magistrate under the code of criminal process may be exercised by the commissioner/superintendent of police and certain other authorities with the permission of the state government. Additionally, it discusses the authority granted to the police by other Acts.

Taking control of unclaimed property and further disposing of it are topics covered in *Chapter IX*.

Forensic Research & Criminology International Journal (2016) .http://medcraveonline.com/FRCIJ/FRCIJ-03-100091.pdf (last visited on 22nd Aug 2018).

[114] Law Commission, Law Commission Of India One Hundred And Thirteen Report On Injuries In Police Custody, Report Number 113th (1985).

[115] Law Commission, Implementation of 'United Nations Convention against Torture and other Cruel, Inhuman and Degrading Treatment or Punishment through Legislation, Report Number 273th (2017).

2: The Police Act 1888

A change was made to the Police Act of 1861 with the Police Act of 1888. The main goal of this amendment was to improve the structure of the Indian police force. The Act granted the State government the authority to create a Police Establishment Board for the purpose of selecting, promoting, moving, and disciplining police officers. The Act also authorised the appointment of a provincial Inspector General of Police.

The Criminal Investigation Department (CID) was one of the major modifications brought about by the Police Act of 1888. The CID was created to carry out specialised investigations into heinous crimes like terrorism, murder, and dacoity. The Act also provided the police extra authority to uphold the law and order in the nation.

The Police Act of 1888 was a significant step in the direction of the professionalisation of the Indian police service overall. It offered the police a better organisational framework and more authority to uphold law and order.

An important piece of law passed by the British Indian government in India during colonial rule was the Police Act of 1888. This Act, which superseded the earlier Police Act of 1861, marked a significant improvement in the way India's police system operated. All of British India's provinces and presidencies were covered by the Act.

The Police Act of 1888 was primarily intended to improve the management and oversight of the Indian police force. It sought to create a more centralised police system and guarantee that the police operated more effectively and efficiently. The Act established a police Commissionerate structure, which is still in use in a number of Indian states today.

The police's duties and authority were spelt out in detail by the Police Act of 1888. The Act set forth the obligations of the police in upholding law and order, combating crime, and defending citizens' rights. Additionally, it called for the creation of police training facilities, whose job it was to educate and train police officers.

Additionally, the Act established the idea of police accountability. It allowed for the selection of a police complaint authority, whose job it was to look into complaints about police officers and take appropriate action against them.

Overall, the Police Act of 1888 represented a considerable advancement in the way India's police system operated. It created the foundation for a more centralised, accountable police force.

3: The Police (Incitement to Disaffection) Act, 1922

In India, the Police (Incitement to Disaffection) Act, 1922, makes it illegal to foment discontent among police officials. Anyone who tries to provoke police officers to refuse their services or violate company policy would be punished under the act. Such actions are subject to a fine, a period of imprisonment that can last up to three years, or both. The act was enacted to stop police officers from being encouraged to take part in actions that would be harmful to the safety and order of the public.

The Mumbai Police filed a FIR against journalists from the Republic Media network earlier this year under Section 3 of the Police (Incitement to Disaffection) Act, 1922. This pre-Constitutional law is rarely invoked, thus it does not frequently make the news or come up in discussions among supporters of constitutional law.

The FIR against the Republic journalists will undoubtedly intensify debates about this law and its potential constitutional ramifications, nevertheless. There are just six provisions in this law, the penal provision being Section 3, which reads as follows:

"*3. Punishment for inciting discontent*, etc.—Whoever intentionally results in, attempts to result in, or does any act that is likely to result in disaffection towards the government establishment among members of a police force, or induces or attempts to induces or does any act that is likely to induce any member of a police force to withhold his services or to commit a breach of discipline, is punishable by imprisonment that may extend to six months, or by fine.

Explanation - Expressions of disapproval of the government's policies with a view to having them changed through legal means, or of disapproval of any administrative or other action taken by the government, do not violate this section unless they result in, are made with the intention of, or are likely to result in disaffection.

It follows that the violation of this clause constitutes a double offence. First off, it is now illegal for police officers in India to incite animosity towards the legally created government. The act is considered punishable if it causes or is likely to cause a member of the police force to refuse to perform their duties or violate departmental policies.

The main element of the Section 3 offence is "disaffection." The term *"disaffection"* makes us think of Section 124-A of the Indian Penal Code, also known as the law that makes sedition illegal. Both Sections 124-A and Section 3 of the Penal Code, which both punish arousing dissatisfaction, have similar phrasing.

In the case of *Kedar Nath Singh* v. *State of Bihar*, where the constitutionality of Section 124-A was in question, the Supreme Court maintained the provision's legality. Conflicting rulings from the Privy Council and the Federal Court about the definition of the word "disaffection" were presented to the court in Kedar Nath[116]. The Court limited the application of the aforementioned provision, taking note of Article 19(2), to only those acts that have the potential to instigate violence, cause unrest, or disturb law and order. The constitutionality of Section 124-A was upheld by applying this interpretation.

In his blog post on this decision, Gautam Bhatia expresses his opinion that the Court in Kedar Nath has added a requirement of concrete evidence of actual injury to the concept of sedition.

Indulal Yagnik, an Ahmedabad-based Lok Sabha member, contested the constitutionality of Section 3 of the Police Act before the Bombay High Court in the case Indulal Yagnik v. State. He was accused of violating Section 3 of the Police Act for comments he allegedly made about police officers during a public address. He was thus charged under the stated section. Later, he filed a petition with the Bombay High Court contesting Section 3's constitutionality.

The restriction wasn't covered by any of the clauses in Article 19(2), and it had a very broad scope, making it subject to the vice of unreasonableness. These were the two main reasons for challenge presented to the Court. The Court acknowledged the validity of this clause while also noting that the phrase "in the interests of public order" would protect the statute. The Court noted the usage of the phrase "in the interests of" as opposed to "for the maintenance of" in Article 19(2) and the fact that "in the interests of" was more general than "for the maintenance of."

---

[116] Law Commission, Law Relating to Arrest, Report No. 177 (2001).

Therefore, it was decided that the said phrase would protect any action that was helpful in maintaining public order. It's interesting to note that neither a thorough examination of the meaning of the word "disaffection" nor an attempt to precisely define the parameters of the aforementioned provision was made in this judgement.

Three years after the Bombay High Court's decision in Indulal Yagnik, the Supreme Court issued its ruling in Kedar Nath. The Supreme Court's interpretation of "disaffection" and its restriction of the scope of Section 124-A of the Penal Code are directly applicable to Section 3 of the Police Act.

There have been ground-breaking advancements in India's free speech law even after the Supreme Court's Kedar Nath decision. In the past, courts were hesitant to invalidate clauses because of how broadly they were framed. Instead, the courts would clarify the meaning of the disputed provisions. This is demonstrated by the Court's strategy in the Kedar Nath case.

Furthermore, the Court rarely heard arguments that a law has a "chilling effect" on free speech. The pattern has since shifted, though. In *Shreya Singhal* v. *Union of India*, the supreme court used the concepts of overbreadth, ambiguity, and chilling impact for the first time to invalidate *Section 66-A* of the Information Technology Act, 2000. It noticed,

Undoubtedly, the overbreadth and chilling impact of Section 3 of the Police Act make it subject to dispute. The Supreme Court has acknowledged the chilling effect in Puttaswamy and Navtej Singh Johar as a way to assess whether a statute restricting a fundamental right is legitimate. Therefore, if a challenge to the Police Act's validity is made, it will be difficult to advance.

This colonial law has another intriguing aspect to it. It is important to highlight right away that colonial laws do not enjoy the same presumption of legitimacy as laws created in an independent India. In the colonial era, where democratic ideals had no place, the police force represented the authority of the colonial State. It was important to punish any provocation of disaffection towards the State or any inducement to violate discipline among police officers because they served as the State's sanctioning arm. "

Additionally, the Law Commission had advocated for the complete repeal of the Police Act in its 248th report from October 2014. According to the aforementioned *Law*

Commission report, the Police Act restrains the right to free speech and has to be reviewed in light of the potential violation of Articles 19(1)(a) and (b) of the Indian Constitution. Furthermore, it was noted that the aforementioned Act is open to abuse.

As was already said, the Court in Kedar Nath decided that in order to prove an offence under Section 124-A, there must be a propensity to instigate public disorder or a propensity to commit an offence. Simple dissatisfaction would not be adequate. The tendency to instigate unrest after inciting feelings of dissatisfaction must be proven, just as it must in the case of an alleged violation of Section 124-A and Section 3 of the Police Act.

Such a tendency must also be close to the accused speech that generates disaffection or encourages discipline violations. The offence cannot be proven if the alleged speech that created the inducement is too far removed from the discipline violation, tendency to commit discipline violation, or public disorder. It will need to be read down in this way if Section 3 is to in any way pass constitutional muster.

4: The Police Act, 1949

An essential piece of legislation that controls how India's police forces operate is the Police Act, 1949. The Police Act of 1861 was repealed in favour of the new law. The Act outlines the creation, management, and regulation of the Indian police forces as well as the responsibilities and authority of police personnel.

According to the Act, the state government is given the authority to oversee all police operations within a state, and the state's director general of police (DGP) is responsible for overseeing police operations. The Act also calls for the creation of a body to investigate complaints made against police officers.

The Act outlines the obligations and responsibilities of police officers, such as maintaining public order, preventing and identifying crime, and protecting people and property.

It also outlines the authority that police officers have, including the authority to make arrests, conduct searches and seizures, and conduct investigations into crimes.

The Act also outlines the establishment of institutes for police training and the regulation of that training. It also outlines the process for hiring, moving, and promoting police personnel.

The Police Act of 1949 has undergone periodic revisions to meet new issues affecting the police force as well as adapt to society's evolving requirements. The creation of the National Police Commission in 1977 and the inclusion of measures for community policing and human rights in 2006 are two of the most significant modifications.

5: The Delhi Special Police Establishment Act 1946

A special police force will be established under the Delhi Special Police Establishment Act, 1946, to look into and stop public servant corruption and other offences. The 1946 DSPE Act is the name given to the legislation, which was passed at the time.

The Central Bureau of Investigation (CBI), India's top investigative organisation, was established under the DSPE Act. The Ministry of Personnel, Public Grievances and Pensions of the Government of India has administrative control over the CBI.

Investigating cases of corruption, economic crimes, and other sophisticated crimes is the CBI's main goal. Additionally, the CBI supports state police agencies in matters of major national and international relevance.

The DSPE Act also calls for the creation of special courts to hear matters that the CBI has looked into. These tribunals, also referred to as the Special CBI tribunals, are authorised to hear matters involving the 1988 Prevention of Corruption Act and other relevant statutes.

Overall, the DSPE Act has made a substantial contribution to India's efforts to combat corruption and other crimes committed by public employees.

However, there have been complaints about the CBI's operation and independence, and there have been proposals for reforms to the CBI's operations.

CHAPTER 8
CONCLUSION AND SUGGESTIONS, RECOMMENDATIONS

The security force is accountable for maintaining law and order in neighbourhoods, ensuring public safety, and safeguarding the agency's image. India's Preamble makes it very plain that no one is above the rules. Additionally, security officers are unlikely to exert undue discipline or misuse their powers in order to harass civilians when conducting an inquiry. The security force is one of the most powerful organizations in society. And it just so happens that the security are the government's most visible officials. In an hour of danger, hazard, tragedy, and difficulty, when a person is unsure what to do or who to contact, the security department and a security officer are often the most suitable and capable unit and entity. Security are expected to be the most approachable, social, and dynamic entity of any community.

In the one side, it is normal for their roles, obligations, and tasks within community to vary; on the other hand, it is challenging. Generally speaking, the security's primary duties are to uphold the rules and maintain justice. However, these two tasks have various implications, necessitating a comprehensive inventory of the security organization's obligations, functions, forces, positions, and responsibilities. Through vesting security officers with a variety of powers and still requiring them to perform their tasks, we open the door to abuse and, therefore, human rights abuses.[117]

Security officers are the first point of communication with residents. The security must maintain peace to deter crime. It is their responsibility to get the suspects to the judge to prosecute them.

The primary goal of the security in Indian society is to preserve public safety, to deter and detain violence, to uphold the rule of law, and to protect human integrity.

Security arrest abilities are restricted and subjected to judicial supervision and review in order to protect everyone's human right to life under Article 21 of the Indian Constitution. Enforcing those limits expressly demonstrates an understanding of the accuser's rights.

Chapter-V of the Criminal Procedure Act (CrPC) includes rules governing the prosecution, detention, and surveillance of individuals, as well as their oversight. The primary objectives of criminal law are punishment, punishment, and security.

---

[117] S.C. Sarkar, Commentary on Code of Criminal Procedure 122-123 (1973)

Transformation and redemption are the covert goals of societal improvement. "Once a Criminal, Always a Criminal," is outside the pale of rationality, intellect, and morals. Not all offenses are the same, and so not all criminals are the same. The weight, nature, and appearance of an object define the applicable jurisprudential rule standard. The yardstick's use, though, is contingent on the exercising of independence within the framework of applicable state laws.

The rule of law is a basic precept of democracy. It states that no one is above the rules and that everybody is fair in front of the law. The rule of law entails fair rights under the law and the lack of legislative unconstitutional forces.[118]

Security forces are critical in upholding and enforcing the rules, resolving criminal offenses, and ensuring protection for the country's inhabitants. In a vast and populous country like India, security forces must be well-maintained in respect of personnel arms, forensic aid, communications, and transportation.[119]

Security expenditures accounted for about 3% of all government budgets. Although state security forces are responsible for maintaining law and order and prosecuting suspects, federal governments provide them with information and assistance with national security matters (e.g., insurgency). Security budgets account for about 3% of federal and state government funding. In January 2016, state protection had a vacancy rate of 24%. (About 5.5 lakh vacancies). And, although the authorized size of the security force was 181 officers per lakh citizens in 2016, the actual force size was 137 officers. Bear in mind that the United Nations proposes 222 security officers for every lakh population. The constabulary employs 86 percent of the security department's Section 29 of the Indian Security Act, 1861 provides that if an individual commits wrongdoing as a result of a security officials failure to perform his or her duties, the officer can be disciplined by up to three months' incarceration and a three-month pay penalty.[123]

If a citizen is called as a victim or as a petitioner, the law enforcement official shall seek a written warrant pursuant to Section 160 of the Code of Criminal Practice, 1973, specifying the date and period of involvement.

---

[118] Steele, W.W., The Doctrine of Right to counsel: its impact on the Administrative Criminal Justice and Legal Profession, south-western L.J. and Sudha Sindhuv. Emperor, op. cit. 107.

[119] S.N.Misra, The Code of Criminal Procedure548 (Central Law Publications, Allahabad, 2006).

However, an attorney can accompany you to the security station to file a complaint against a securityman.[124]

In the case of a security arrest, you may be aware of two documents: the quest document and the arrest memorandum. An assessment memorandum is critical when it details your appearance prior to being trapped and if you had any injuries prior to being locked up or not, so that you should not sustain an injury through the inquiry. The Memorandum of Detention contains detailed information regarding the crime, namely eyewitness identities, and there are no fabricated statements from the security side.

Several efforts have been taken over the last three decades to implement significant security changes. Between 1978 and 1981, the National Security Commission released eight reports with a variety of recommendations but took little action to implement them. The Apex Court recognized the urgent need to implement these reforms in *Vineet Narain v. Union of India*[120], prompting the Ribeiro Committee to send two reports in 1998 and 1999; the Central Government named the *Padmanabhaiah Committee Report in 2000 and the Mali math Committee Report in 2002*[121].

The directives involve the following: each Local Authority shall constitute a Government Security Committee to safeguard security against unlawful political power, namely specifying the selection and necessary duration of the Chief of Security (DGP); the required duration of other law enforcement officials including the Inspector General of Security (IGP), Deputy Inspector General of Security (Deputy IGP), District Supreme Security (DSP), and Station Security man; and Establish a Security Equality Committee. Due to the limited reach of this document, we will limit our topic to the Security Investigations Body.[122]

The Indian Constitution and regulatory legislation provide public law accountability for law enforcement. For violations of fundamental rights enshrined in Part III of the Constitution, such as the life and personal liberty, security against unreasonable searching and false detention, and protection against injustice and unequal care the judges have

---

[120] (1998) 1 SCC 226
[121] Supra
[122] M.L. Updadhaya, "Torture in Police Custody and Handcuffing of the Accused", Central Indian Law Quarterly, Vol. IXLIV, 458 (1996).

routinely held the security accountable under civil law and imposed pecuniary liability on the State as penalty for the resulting injury.[123]

The precedence dates all the way back to 1983, when, in *Rudul Sah* v. *the State of Bihar,*[124] a three-judges Apex Court bench acting on lawful approval issued an injunction of compensation for violations of Indian Constitution *Articles 21 and 22*. In this scenario, too, the perpetrator was wrongfully imprisoned for 14 years after his acquittal. Since concluding that his arrest was entirely unjustified, he sought relief for the arbitrary arrest.

In the instance of *State of Maharashtra* v. *Ravi Kant Patil[132]*, a prisoner on tribunal was handcuffed, his arms were linked with a chain, and he was marched down the roads, exposing himself to scorn and outrage. According to Rudul Shah[125], the Apex Court upheld the High Court's decision that the State Government must incur a charge of Rs 10,000. Even so, the court thought about whether to hold the individual law enforcement official accountable or to order the state to compensate the charge. The court recalled, in reasoning for momentary blame, that "he simply acted as an officer and also felt he had met his limits, and so refrained in removing the handcuffs of the under-trials inmates."[126]

In PUCL v. *Union of India*[127], the Apex Court considered whether the State may deprived a citizen of his existence and privileges in violation of a statute's law and then claims immunity on the grounds that the oppression occurred when Law enforcement officials exerted legislative power. Contrary of what the Court determined. The court determined in the case of *Nilabati Behara* that a cash payout is an appropriate and thereby effective remedy in the event that a citizen's fundamental right to liberty is violated by a State public officer who is vicariously liable for their behavior.[128]

Following a review of the preceding precedents, the following points become apparent:

[123] M.S. Balwinder Kumar, "Protection against Torture by Police", The PRP Journal of Human Rights, Oct-Dec 15 (2002).
[124] {1983 (4) SCC 141} 132 Rao, P. Srikrishna Deva. "RETROGRESSIVE STEP IN COMPENSATORY JURISPRUDENCE: A CRITIQUE OF STATE OF MAHARASHTRA V. RAVIKANT S. PATIL." Journal of the Indian Law Institute 34.3 (1992): 472-474.
[125] Supra
[126] Ibid.
[127] AIR 1978 SC 1025.
[128] J.N.Pandey, Constitution law of India222(2007)

1. It is self-evident that, in addition to criminal and civil law, a violation of civil rights including excessive misconduct would result in public law responsibility.

2. Financial responsibility for such a violation of human rights should be created.

3. Since the Government is kept accountable, the State bears the cost, not the specific security men considered negligent.

4. The Apex Court determined that a high standard of evidence was required to establish security misconduct such as harassment, intimidation, and custodial assault, and to hold the State accountable for the same. The remedy should be accessible only for egregious and irrefutable violations of human rights.

5. Since the principle of full privilege does not apply to situations including violations of civil rights, it cannot be seen as a legal defense.

6.1. Suggestions

The CrPC provides legal safeguards to governmental officials under criminal investigation in attempt to help prevent scurrilous litigation against an officer that is performing a public function. Officials working in security were found to be protected by Section 197 of the Criminal Procedure Code, a broader section, and Section 132 of the Criminal Procedure Code, a narrower section.

The section above notes that subsequent to taking disciplinary action against a protection officer suspected of performing a criminal crime, "whether the act was done in his professional capacity or as a private citizen," approval from the National or Local Authority is needed. The civil suit filed by P.P. Unnikrishnan against the deputy superintendent of the prison under which he was being kept in Alikutty (Punjab) is one in which two policemen were accused of wrongly imprisoning and tormenting a petitioner for several days.

In light of the need to maintain order in the state of Kerala, the Apex Court constitution benches had to contend with the constitutional privileges of security personnel outlined in Section 64 of the Kerala Security Act, which forbids the initiation of judicial cases against security personnel operating in good faith due to their responsibility under any jurisdiction or requirement levied by the state legislature.

The conclusions drawn from the preceding results are applicable to the case at hand. The introductory paragraph of this explanation states that substantive protection under Section 197 CrPC is applicable only if the convicted security policeman is willing to prove that the suspected criminal activity was performed while carrying out an authorized function.

In an order to find out why it is required to penalize security personnel for charging them, it is important to take into consideration the specifics of the acts the accused officer performed when conducting his or her duties. Secondly, the issue of whether the activity is applicable to the protection obligation is not quite as relevant as whether the criterion for deciding whether the action took place when the officer was doing their duties.

Section 46 of the Criminal Procedure Code examines several means of incarceration, including surrender to custody, physical treatment of the body, and confinement. Arrest is a violation of civil rights. When anyone is imprisoned, whether by words or acts, physical contact can have an effect on their incarceration. Where force is used, it should be used sparingly, since this law does not give the authority to impose death on anyone who is not threatened with a capital or life-threatening offense. Where an individual is to be arrested, the security officer shall not make communication with her body because the officer is a woman who would be presumed to be arrested upon her admission to detention on verbal implied threat.

Section 50(1) of the Criminal Procedure Code states that "any security officer or other suspect capturing an individual without a summons shall immediately report to him the full particulars of the offense for which he is being detained or any other excuse for such detention." Besides the requirements of the CrPC,

Article 22(1) of the Indian Constitution states that "No individual detained shall be kept in confinement without being informed of the grounds for his restraint as soon as practicable, nor shall he be denied the right to contact and support a lawyer of his choice." Based on the Apex Court rulings in *Joginder Kumar v. The State of Uttar Pradesh,* [137], and *D.K. Basu* v *The State of West Bengal*, [138], significant changes to Section 50-A of the CrPC were introduced, requiring the law enforcement official who makes an arrest to notify the detained individual's acquaintance, parent, or other candidate of his detention, to notify the arresting security man of his privileges, and to write the arrested person's name on the security registry. Thus, the prosecutor is required to keep himself informed of security activity.

Section 41 of the CrPC vests security men with extraordinary abilities to arrest, particularly in perpetrated offences, without the need to approach a Magistrate and obtain an apprehension order. There can be no legitimate detention where there is no proof of reasonable suspicion that the suspect has committed a cognizable crime or committed the offence(s) specified in Section 41. The security officer is responsible for convincing the judge that he or she has a reasonable basis for doubting the arrest. Except as given above, Section 45 of the CrPC prohibits arresting representatives of the Armed Forces for anything undertaken in the execution of professional functions without the permission of the centralized administration. *Section 54 of the CrPC* provides for mandatory medical examinations conducted by a clinical professional employed by the state or national governments, or by a qualified clinical professional in the absence of a health examiner Women arrestees can be treated by only female security officers or qualified medical professionals. However, Sections 53 and 53A of the CrPC provide that where there are reasonable reasons to believe that an examination of a convicted individual on charges of abuse or any offence would reveal signs of the commission of such crime, it is permissible to examine the blood, blood stains, semen, hair extracts, and fingernail marks utilizing new and revolutionary methods such as DNA.

Section 49 of the CrPC notes that there can be no further restraint that is reasonably necessary to prevent escaping, i.e. reasonable force can be utilized to accomplish the task; nevertheless, an apprehension must occur prior to an individual being placed under a form of restriction.

Seizing or prosecuting without arrest is illegal. *Section 50(2)* of the Criminal Procedure Code requires that any individual detained without summons be notified promptly of the cause for his detention and, if the investigation is done in a pardonable situation, of his ability to be granted bail. Section 50 is mandatory and complies with Article 22(1) of the Indian Constitution.

It is critical to strictly adhere to civil and legal provisions regarding the presentation of an arrested party before a Magistrate Court within 24 hours of detention *(Khatri v. State of*

Bihar[139]). Section 57 is solely concerned with the detention time. The aim is to get the criminal to a qualified judge as soon as possible for trial or conviction. The ability to be freed from criminal detention by appearing before a judge is critical in order to prevent arrest and incarceration for the purpose of collecting testimony or coercing people to provide proof.

The security's abuse of policing authority has a detrimental effect on the civil rights of victims of personal injury offenses[129].

When victims' rights to life are threatened or intimidated, the right to defense is breached, and the victim may need assistance from government apparatus.[140]

The freedom to seek justice is harmed where plaintiffs' cases are either not recorded or are postponed for one reason or another, or when they are recorded, the details are distorted to change the essence of the situation, even when the Section intended to be applied is not invoked in order to demonstrate reduction of offenses. Occasionally, in order to protect the survivors of violence, specific individuals are prevented.[141] Criminal victims have a right to an impartial inquiry.

Proper investigation is essential to guarantee a proper hearing. The Courts may only ascertain the facts of a crime perpetrated by individuals by an interpretation of the facts gathered by a reasonable and equitable inquiry[130].

After analyzing the many ways in which the inquiry has been abused and its impact on the victim's civil rights.

a. Every three years, the national regulatory structure, which contains Security Acts, Policing Documents, and regulations pertaining to investigations in the Code of Criminal Procedure, should be revised to ensure alignment with Global Quality Management for the law enforcement system.

b. The human right of survivors to redress should be respected, alongside the State's duty to provide justice. To do this, the Document should be changed to include

---

[129] Prof. N. V. Paranjape, Criminology & Penology with Victimology , Sixteenth Edition 2014 - chapter XVll, The Police System
[130] S. M. A. Qadri, Criminology & Penology, Chapter-X-The Police, Sixth Edition, 2009

articles enforcing the Victims' Human Right to Justice explicitly. Both State departments would take strictly this fundamental right.

c. Victim-specific laws should be enacted to spell out in more depth the protections that victims of abuse have; the recourse open to them in the event of a breach of those rights; the process to be taken seeking recompense; and whom they should approach in the event of a breach

d. A framework for victim-witness safety may be established by the enactment of special laws or the incorporation of specific laws into the Indian Penal Code and the Code of Criminal Procedure where victims may assert their rights to immunity.

e. To avoid victim coercion or actual danger to safety, 'pre-event solutions' should be given in accordance with international quality standards. Communication between the defendant and the claimant (or otherwise) may be viewed as an irritating situation. In any situations of domestic abuse a default restraint order should be imposed against the defendant.

f. An alternate method for the source to file the F.I.R. could be formulated to avoid contact with the authorities at the point.

g. At any critical point of the case, the survivor should be told of the actions taken so far, with a version being submitted to the Judge. If any detail needs to be omitted, it should be stated in the document to the Magistrate, together with justifications. The Code of Criminal Procedure may be revised to include certain statutes, as well as a legislative redress for violations of this right.

h. Upon conclusion of the inquiry, the officer-in-duty would submit his document to the judge for consideration. Additionally, the officer is expected to warn the source of his or her behavior in such case.

Only the source has a privilege under Section 173 (2) (ii). The security man is not required to warn the victim or his relatives about his behavior. To protect situations in which the informant is not the victim or a spouse, Section 173 (2) (ii) may be updated to ensure that not only the source, but also the offender or, in the situation of a dead suspect, his close relatives are eligible to obtain certain material.

In conclusion, India's police system has a lengthy history and has undergone substantial development.

In India, the police play a critical role in enforcing the criminal justice system, protecting citizens, and preserving law and order. However, the Indian police force has had to contend with a number of issues, including political meddling, a lack of proper training, and out-of-date laws.

In an effort to address these issues and implement police reforms, numerous groups and judicial interventions have been formed. A significant ruling by the Supreme Court in the Prakash Singh case provided guidelines for ensuring police accountability and independence. The implementation of these reforms, however, continues to be difficult, and ongoing work is required to significantly alter how the police system operates in India.

To ensure that it acts within the bounds of the law and advances the interests of the populace, the police system must be continuously improved and reformed. The police must strive to earn the confidence of the public by carrying out their tasks and obligations in a just, unbiased, and effective manner.

The Indian Penal Code of 1860, the Code of Criminal Procedure of 1973, and the Indian Evidence Act of 1972 all play important roles in the criminal justice system in India. However, the police frequently go against the guidelines outlined in numerous criminal statutes in their job.

While the Criminal Procedure Code covers any regulations relating to crimes and criminals, the Indian Penal Code specifies crimes and punishments. The law forbids the police from harassing or coercing suspects, using foul language, filing a false police report, or engaging in illegal detention, but the police continue to engage in this despised practise everywhere.

The SC occasionally provides guidelines for the police to carry out their duties in a proper manner, but there is a greater need to abide by the laws that are set forth in order to establish the role of the police in the criminal justice system in order to maintain law and order without violating human rights.

Rather of creating laws, officers are tasked with upholding and implementing the rule of law. When security officials are granted actual power, they must be held accountable for the wrongs they do since this departure from past and present conventions will require their isolation and substantive autonomy from illegitimate authority and outside intervention.

It is necessary to enhance and upgrade the current governmental structures. Alternative methods for monitoring security activity and looking into citizen complaints about security must also be developed. Constant supervision is required of the security department's overall performance as well as the actions of specific personnel.

The alternative is to make every practical effort, within the constraints of the existing framework and procedure, to improve and strengthen policing.

Officers are entrusted with upholding and enforcing the rule of law rather than making new laws. Since this departure from past and present conventions will require their isolation and substantive autonomy from illegitimate authority and outside intervention, security officials who are given actual power must be held accountable for the wrongs they commit.

The current governmental structures must be improved and updated. It's also important to develop alternative techniques for keeping track of security activity and investigating security-related complaints from the public. The acts of specific employees as well as the general performance of the security department must be constantly monitored.

The alternative is to take all reasonable steps to enhance and improve policing while staying within the bounds of the currently in place framework and procedure.

BIBLIOGRAPHY

1. C:/Users/User/Downloads/advocacy_paper_police_act_1861.pdf

2. file:///C:/Users/User/Downloads/01_The_Police_Act_1861.pdf

3. file:///C:/Users/User/Downloads/SSRN-id3113282.pdf

4. file:///C:/Users/User/Downloads/Police_Reforms.pdf

5. file:///C:/Users/User/Downloads/40-Article%20Text-132-1-10-20210706.pdf

6. file:///C:/Users/User/Downloads/GGSIPU_USLLS_ILR_2020_V1-I2-010-Dr_Mudasir_Bhat_Dr_Mehraj_Ud_Din_Mir-1.pdf

7. http://ssglawfirm.in/police-act-1861-and-model-police-act-2006-an-analysis/

Books

8. Bakshi, Parvinrai Mulwantrai, and Subhash C. Kashyap. The constitution of India. Universal Law Publishing, 1982.

9. Doak, J. (2008). The victim in criminal law and justice.

10. Karmen, Andrew. Crime victims: An introduction to victimology. Cengage Learning, 2015.

11. Prakash, Abhinav. Code of Criminal Procedure. Universal Law Publishing, 2007

12. Dr. Avtar Singh, Principles Of The Law Of Evidence, Central Law Publications, 2020

13. Bandyopadhyay, Rekha. "Land system in India: A historical review." Economic and Political Weekly (1993): A149-A155.

14. Halabi, S. F. (2013). Constitutional Borrowing as Jurisprudential and Political Doctrine in Shri DK Basu v. State of West Bengal. Notre Dame J. Int'l & Comp. L., 3, 73.

15. Singh, Jasmine K. "Everything I'm Not Made Me Everything I Am: The Racialization of Sikhs in the United States." Asian Pac. Am. LJ 14 (2008): 54.

16. Rao, P. Hari. "The Indian Police Act (Act V of 1861)." (1927).

17. Sherman, Lawrence W., ed. Police corruption: A sociological perspective. Garden City: Anchor Press, 1974.

18. David, Saul. The Indian Mutiny: 1857. Penguin UK, 2003.

Articles :

19. Rakesh Mohan, Police and Human Rights6 (Swastika Publications, N.Delhi, 2013).

20. Verma, Arvind. "National Police Commission in India: An analysis of the policy failures." The Police Journal 71.3 (1998): 226-244.

21. Garg, Pooja. "Shifting Trends in Burden of Proof and Standard of Proof: An Analysis of the Malimath Committee Report." Student B. Rev 17 (2005): 38.

22. Haritas, K., 2020. Law made injustice possible in Ayodhya, Hyderabad encounter cases. Will this happen with CAA too?.

23. Karol, S. (2015). Bifurcation of the Indian Police System: Investigation Wing and Law & Order Maintenance Wing. Available at SSRN 2601997.

24. Dalbir Bharti, Police and People, Role and Responsibilities 76 (APH Publishing House, New Delhi, 2006).

25. Baier, P. R. (2015). From Magna Carta to Chambers v. Florida: Hugo Black and "the law of the land.".

26. Stephen, James Fitzjames. The Indian Evidence Act (I. of 1872): with an introduction on the principles of judicial evidence. Macmillan and Company, 1872.

27. Aston, J. N. (2020). Torture Behind Bars: Role of the Police Force in India. Oxford University Press.

28. Dr. Deepa Singh, Human Rights and Police Predicament 59(The Bright Law House Delhi, 2002).

29. John S Dempsy, linda. S.Frost, An Introduction to Policing 4 (Thomson Wordsworth, CA, USA, 3rdedn).

30. Shani, Ornit. Communalism, caste and Hindu nationalism: The violence in Gujarat. Cambridge University.